❖ *My Last Breath* ❖

MEG SECHREST

Britni,

Hope you enjoy the book

Happy Reading

M Sechrest

Meg Sechrest

First Printing, 2018
ISBN 9781729136270
www.CreateSpace.com
Create Space Publishing is a division of Amazon and Kindle Direct Publishing.
Printed in the United States of America

Meg Sechrest

For the United States Armed Forces and anyone who's ever loved and lost.

PROLOGUE

"The preacher's ready. Come on, love."

Melanie turned to face her mother and draped the tiny black veil over her face before she exited the back of the car.

Shakily, she stood and looked around at all the people in the wooded cemetery.

"No, Mama. I can't do this. I can't even breathe." Sobs began slowly, then continued forcefully, but her mother held her arm and led her along toward the rows of chairs in front of the casket as she cried.

"You *can* do this because you have to," her mother said as they approached the dark box, walking past her friends and family members, who'd parted and taken their seats in order to allow her access through. But the sight of it was too much for her and she dropped to her knees.

"No!" she cried out, dropping her face, placing her hands above her on the smooth, shiny wood, then moving her fingers to grip the flag that had been draped across. "This can't be real," she continued, tears dripping from her cheeks and pounding onto the grass below. "Come back to me. I don't know what to do." Her sobs worsened, pleading for anything else in the world to be a reality, except this.

ONE

"Melanie? Are you ready? My sister isn't going to wait all night!" Amber hollered, as she put the finishing touches on her makeup.

"Almost ready! Give me two minutes!" Melanie hollered back. Knowing she was going to be meeting college guys that night, she wanted to be sure she was looking her best. One last touch to her mascara and lip gloss, then a tug on her halter top and a toss at her loose curls, and she was on her way.

"Where are we meeting Kaylee?" Melanie asked as they hurried out the front door.

"There's a bar that my brother and some friends of his like to frequent when they come into town."

"Your brother... as in the one who's about to graduate from Yale?" she asked.

"Yeah, James. He's really smart and he's been attending Yale for some kind of smart guy thing, but he's really nice and totally down to earth. Don't feel intimidated by him," Amber said.

Melanie let out a "Huh," but just got into the front seat of Amber's car and fastened her seatbelt, readying herself for their pre-graduation celebration.

Amber's older sister, Kaylee, and a couple of her friends were waiting outside in the smoker's section of the Atlanta bar when they arrived.

"Hi!" Amber waved as they walked up.

"Hey! Everyone else is inside, but I'll take you in and introduce you to them," Kaylee said as she tossed her cigarette down and walked inside to the far corner of the bar where her brother was waiting with some friends.

Amber and Kaylee were average southern girls with enough sass to melt molasses in a northern winter, but they were also sweeter than sugar, like typical southerners, which drew Melanie to liking them.

Melanie had grown up a spoiled, upper-class, northern girl with a lot of sophistication and charm, always attending garden parties of her mother's, and yacht club events for her father's pharmacy, until their divorce moved her to the heart of southern living with unsophisticated honky tonks everywhere and not a sushi bar for as far as she could see. Plus, now she was adjusting to life in a split home, which only made everything worse. But the sisters' happy-go-lucky attitudes—which were much different from her own, as she was used to being reserved in nature, mostly—were keeping her satisfied.

Amber was lively and outgoing, cheeky and lippy; Kaylee was snarky and sarcastic, but Melanie, however, was raised to mind her manners. And it seemed like everyone down here behaved like they just walked out of a barn. Tonight, Amber was wearing cut-off jean shorts, an old tank top which was tied up in a knot on the side, and cow-girl boots, and she had her shoulder-length brown hair with highlights, pulled up in a messy bun on the top of her head, and was wearing far too much make-up. Kaylee, similarly, was in jean shorts, but had on a t-shirt with the University of Tennessee logo on it. But her brown hair was a little longer and was pulled to the sides of her head in two pig tails. Looking at the sisters, Melanie was feeling very out of place in her strappy satin tank and jeans, but also by having her brown hair down and curled nicely.

"This is my sometimes boyfriend, Willis, and he's also my brother's best friend," Kaylee started introducing around the table, pointing to each person respectively. "Y'all know my sister Amber. This is Melanie. Melanie, this is everyone. And *that's* my brother James," she said, ending on James when she finished introductions.

Melanie waved, looking around to each person, but her gaze rested on James as his was on her. When everyone scattered to the restrooms or the pool tables, and she took a seat on the bar stool a few places down from him, he was sure to take notice.

Enjoying the pretty image that she was, certain he wanted an introduction, he grabbed up his whiskey sour and headed her way.

"Can I get you a drink?" he asked, leaning against the table.

Blushing deeply, biting her lip, she replied, "Oh. Well, as flattered as I am, I..."

"Are you hitting on my friend?!" Amber exclaimed as she walked up from behind Melanie.

Startled by her words, he spewed the drink in his mouth out and all over Melanie, saying, "She's *your* friend?! I thought she was Kaylee's friend!"

"Ugh. Men and their hormones." Amber rolled her eyes. "No. She's in my senior class. We're graduating together next month. Now keep your peter in his pants. C'mon, Mel. Let's see how we can get you cleaned up."

Taking Melanie's arm, Amber turned to walk away. But James hollered, "Amber, hold on!"

They turned to face him as he reached out, lightly grasping Melanie's fingers.

"I have a t-shirt in my truck she can put on," he offered and pointed behind himself to the side exits, taking a firmer hold of Melanie's fingers, pulling her along as he exited. She smiled, nervously holding his hand the whole way to his truck, hoping he would initiate some sort of conversation, but also admiring how strikingly good-looking she thought he was—with his blonde hair that was shaved short on the sides but longer and combed back on the top, and his large, sparkling blue eyes, that caught her glance from under his long eyelashes, and she felt it hard not to stare at his tall, muscular body as he moved beside her while they walked.

"It's just a t-shirt from my university, but it's better than having my spit, whiskey, and lemon all over you," he said, reaching into his truck, pulling out an old wrinkled-up t-shirt.

"So, Amber tells me you attend Yale?" she asked, as to avoid things getting awkward.

He turned around and held up the t-shirt stamped with a big "Y" and a "Bulldogs" logo, confirming her statement. "That is true," he grinned. "I graduate next year. My sister talks about me?" he wondered.

"Not really. She just mentioned you because I was up there visiting my mom," she said as they walked back inside to the restrooms.

"Parents divorced?" he asked.

"Yeah. That's why I just moved here at the beginning of the school year. I like this weather better than Connecticut and my mom wanted to live there with her new husband, but my dad lives here. I don't really like my mom's new husband, but... Oh! Ouch! So sorry!" she screeched as she tripped over a misplaced barstool and fell right into him.

"No problem," he replied, catching her in his arms and helping her to a stand, liking the small feel he got of her. "The restrooms are right here. I'll wait over there for you."

She walked into the bathroom to put on his shirt, and his eyes were enjoying every moment of watching her walk away, but mostly his thoughts were fixated on her stunning figure and light brown hair as it flowed softly over her shoulders.

"Hey, Melanie," Amber said, as she noticed Melanie walk into the bathroom.

"Oh. Hey," Melanie said, entering a stall to change.

"So, my brother seems pretty enraptured by you," Amber said, while Melanie changed her shirt in the stall and Amber touched up her makeup in the mirror.

"Oh? Why do you say that? I thought he was just being polite," Melanie responded.

"Ha! I know James. James's polite consists of 'Hi. Nice to meet you. Let me get that door for you.' But definitely never 'Here, let me fall all over myself and offer you my favorite shirt that I never take out of my 80,000-dollar truck.' *That's* James, Mel," she said, as Melanie dropped her jaw and peeked her face around the stall.

"You're kidding!" Melanie said.

"Nope. Not at all. He's got the hots for you."

"Not about *that*. I mean about how much he spent for that truck!"

"Oh! Ha! Nope. Totally serious. That's James though," Amber shrugged. "He's super cheap when it comes to everyday purchases, but on big spending he's smart and invests himself wisely. When our Granddaddy died a few years ago and left my daddy a ton of money, we each got some. But Kaylee and I weren't allowed to touch it because we weren't *old* enough, according to my dad. But James is the oldest, so he got his bit."

"And he bought the truck?" Melanie asked.

"Nope. He invested it."

"Wow. He sounds very..."

"Boring?" Amber teased.

"No. I was going to say..."

"Smart? Yeah, yeah, we hear it all the time. Ready?" Amber asked, looking Melanie up and down.

"I guess so." She turned to face the mirror, judging herself in his worn-out Yale t-shirt.

"Where's your bra?" Amber asked.

"I was in a halter top! I don't have one." She sighed, tucking her top into her purse, and pulling the tee up around her waist to tie it in a knot, exposing her bellybutton. "Much better," she grinned, looking to Amber for approval.

"Ha! Well, you'll really give my brother a thrill now! C'mon," Amber joked and tapped Melanie on the shoulder, and they exited the bathroom.

"Where'd James go?" Melanie asked as they walked into the hall.

"He's impatient. You were probably taking too long," she answered as they approached the table and saw James sitting with everyone else. Melanie rolled her eyes and went to sit at the opposite end of the table, but paused at hearing the jukebox turn on— The Charlie Daniel's Band playing— and Willis hollered out, "James! They're playin' your song, boy!"

Melanie watched James gulp down his whiskey, excitement crossing his face.

"Batten down the hatches! The Devil's come down to Georgia, rednecks!" Then he raced over to Melanie and took her hand, saying, "They're playing my song." And she smiled widely at his silly excitement.

He hurried with her over to the center of the bar where there was a floor for dancing, and he began doing a classic country dance, moving and stomping his feet. "The Devil went down to Georgia; he was looking for a soul to steal," James sang, enticing her, provoking her, and challenging her to engage in dancing with him, and as the song played and the words changed, he seduced her to dance along, challenging her to dance against him, until the next part of the song came on.

"The boy said, "My name's Johnny and it might be a sin, but I'll take your bet, you're gonna regret, 'cause I'm the best there's ever been." Melanie sang and danced back, kicking up her feet, dancing, and impressing, and turning on James more than he was willing to admit, and Melanie danced over his way when the next part came on, singing, "Johnny, rosin up your bow and play your fiddle hard, 'cause hell's broke loose in Georgia and the Devil deals the cards, and if you win you'll get this shiny fiddle made of gold, but if you lose, the Devil gets your soul!" And they sang and danced together, until James twirled her back out away from him for the next part and he sang alone.

"The Devil opened up his case and he said, 'I'll start this show." James playfully air guitared to the music and continued his amazing country style dancing, looking to her to continue.

But then Melanie skipped up and flirtatiously pushed him back to a chair singing, "When the Devil finished, Johnny said, well you're pretty good old son but sit down in that chair right there and let me show you how it's done!" and she began doing a fast-paced, Irish step dance, *wowing* James, and he stood just to watch and admire her as she delicately clapped her feet against the dance floor, kicking her legs up high, and spinning around, singing, "Fire on the Mountain, run, boys, run. The Devil´s in the house of the rising sun..."

As the song ended, James smiled and stepped up to her, bowed, extending his hand to her, letting her know that he'd surrendered, and he clapped at her amazing dancing skills, wanting to know how he was going to get her to do that for him again.

Proudly walking over to him, she straightened her posture, nodded and winked, and said, "Did the devil just bow to me?"

He laughed slightly and replied, "I admit I wasn't expecting that. Where'd you learn to dance like that?"

"I know Irish step dancing," she said.

"It was... wow," he replied in a daze.

"You're not so bad yourself though. I wouldn't mind having another go," she said before tapping his chin and turning to walk away. But he reached for her arm and pulled her close, whispering, "Come sit with me," and he held her hand, eagerly leading her along to sit with him.

Everyone had situated themselves around a few large tables in the corner of the room, where she sat closely on his left.

"That was quite the display you two!" Kaylee said.

"Melanie, you're quite the dancer," Willis pointed out.

James looked to him, staking claim, but Willis noticed right away, so he rephrased.

"You must've taken some type of dance lessons?"

"I took Irish step dancing as a kid. It was popular to do where I grew up."

"Well, I've never seen feet move like that before. I don't think James knew what he was up against! You really showed him up! It's time someone did," Willis laughed.

"Willis, you're my brother of another color and we've been best friends for as long as I can remember, but shut the hell up."

Willis looked to James with a wide grin and said, "James, it's okay buddy. I think Melanie here likes that she's the better dancer. From our view, looks to us like she's just as enamored by you as you are by her. If you play your cards right, my friend, you might hit the jackpot." He winked to James and raised his eyebrows playfully to Melanie.

Willis and James had been best friends since elementary school, since Willis moved to Atlanta with his Aunt after his parents were tragically killed in a plane crash. Willis had come from an upper-middle class family in New York, but when he was about 8 years old, his mother and father were traveling together and their plane was in an accident as it was leaving the runway and both his parents were killed, leaving him to live with his only other living relative— his father's sister— in Atlanta. And that's how the never-ending friendship of dark-skinned northerner-turned-southerner, Willis, and southern-living-loving James became best friends.

"He will do no such thing!" Amber said to Willis, then turned to James. "You will not! Jamie, aren't there enough girls your age up at your fancy smart guy's school that you don't need to hit on *my* friends?!"

"Sure there are, but then where's the fun in that?" He grinned, glancing to Melanie who wasn't looking at either of them.

"So, Melanie" Willis hollered across the table. "Amber says you just moved here?"

"Yes. I was living in Connecticut with my mom, but my dad came here for work after their divorce and I decided to come with him and get away from my mom's dreadful new husband."

"Well, I'm sure you'll love it! Southern living is so much better than Yankee living! Just ask James!" Willis nodded with a smirk.

"What's he mean?" Melanie asked, glancing to James.

"Just that I miss being down here." He shrugged. "Want to give me another reason to miss it?" he flirted.

"*Maybe*," she flirted in return.

"Melanie, you're at the top of your graduating class. That's quite an accomplishment for a class of more than 2,000 students," Willis said.

"I am. Right now, I'm third in our class, but I'm hoping to change that with our finals."

Willis nodded and said, "You better stay away from this guy then!" He pointed to James. "He's a terrible influence!"

Melanie smiled slightly, biting her lip, and said, "James, I thought you were the smart one of the Hunter family?"

"But that doesn't mean I'm a *good* boy." He winked at her and hollered for the waitress. "Another whiskey sour, Valerie!" Then he looked to Melanie, "Anything for you?"

"I'll have a sweet tea. Thank you," she answered.

Then he yelled back to the waitress, pointing to Melanie, "And a sweet tea for this cutie!"

"Well, some of us have to work very hard for *our* success in school, James," she teased playfully.

"I work hard too, during the school week. But when the weekend comes..." He winked.

"James! What about that trip to Alabama we've been wanting to take. You game?" Willis said, turning James's attention away from Melanie for a moment, allowing Amber to speak to her.

"Melanie!" she quietly reproved, "You can't be serious!"

Melanie shrugged. "I can't help that your brother is *so* hot and also intelligent. Plus, you're right. He *does* like me!"

Amber groaned and said, "You don't know him like I know him, Mel. He's... Never mind. Find out for yourself. It's your life."

"One whiskey sour for you," the waitress said and laid his drink down in front of him, while obviously brushing up against him.

"Here's your tea," she said, looking to Melanie.

James looked up to her but said nothing. Instead, he scooted his chair closer to Melanie, stretching his arm around her.

His fingers started gently grazing her arm as he rested his elbow on the back of her chair, and his intentions started turning elsewhere while he finished off his whiskey.

"Want my cherry?" he asked, lifting it off the glass, extending it out toward her. "I never eat them."

"Sure," she smiled, biting it off the end while he held the stem in his fingers, and he whispered in her ear, "I'm not asking you out just to piss off my sister, and I know I'm a lot older than you, but let's say you leave here with me tonight?"

Completely taken in by the beauty of his eyes and the way his fingers were teasing her skin as he moved them along her arm, she couldn't say no.

"Okay," she agreed, taking a sip of her tea to wash down the cherry.

"Good. Let's get out of here." He pulled out some money from his wallet, left it on the table for his drinks *and* hers, and took her hand, yanking her up off her chair. Then he said, "We'll see you losers later," saluting his finger from his forehead to mock them.

"Where are you going?!" Amber hollered out, watching Melanie leave with James.

Melanie turned and shrugged, biting her lip as she held his hand and hurried out.

"Where *are* we going?" she asked, as he helped her climb into his gigantic truck.

"I don't know. Away," he replied while he climbed in on his side.

"Oh." She turned to look out the window. "I *should* let you know that..."

"Let me know what?" he interrupted, turning his attentions to her while he drove out of the parking lot.

Avoiding what she was *actually* going to tell him, she changed her thought pattern, since she didn't yet know his intentions with her, and she blurted out, "Your sister hasn't really told me a lot about you, except that you're super smart and that you've obviously invested your money wisely." She motioned around to his expensive truck.

"Alright," he said, focused on the road in front of him.

"Well, I feel like I should *know* things about you. I mean, isn't that what people do on dates?"

He glanced her way, asking, "Have you never *been* on a date before, Melanie?"

Blushing deeply, she replied, "No. But it wasn't for lack of options. I was just being particular."

He chuckled. "I see. Then, why am I so different?" he asked, looking to her with a wide smile.

"I just have a good feeling about you, I suppose. Don't make me regret it," she said.

"You won't regret me," he responded while he pulled the truck down a long dirt road into a wooded area and parked under a large willow tree near a small pond. "Come. I want to show you something," he said, climbing down his side and shutting the door, then hurrying to help her out.

"Where are we?" she asked. Looking around at the small pond that was surrounded by trees, she noticed a small wooden bridge that overstretched the water where there were beautiful lily pads all over.

"I come down here to this park when I'm home. School makes me think on complicated subjects all the time and sometimes I need to let my mind rest, so I come out here and sit just to relax." He walked out to the center and sat with his tall legs over the edge of the bridge and patted the area next to him, encouraging her to join him.

Sitting down beside him, draping her legs over the side, she asked, "What do you study up there in your smart guy's school?"

Smiling slightly, he replied, "I'm studying Aerospace Engineering. I want to be a pilot for NASA someday."

"Oh wow. What an amazing goal," she admired.

"What are your goals for the future?" he asked, watching the moon sparkle off her deep brown eyes and shine crystals off her hair.

"Ha. I'm just hoping to make it out of high school alive," she said.

Curious about that, he asked, "You don't have any dreams you want to pursue?"

"Um... well, nothing compared to NASA. That's pretty spectacular. But I love medicine and I think I'd enjoy a career in something like that someday. But not as a doctor. I'm not quite sure yet."

"So, your mom is in Connecticut but your dad is here? I suppose that explains your *Yankee accent*," he teased, stressing his heavy southern drawl.

"Well, not *everybody* down here talks like a hick. You should be used to it, having been up north for a few years. No?" she said, sticking out her tongue.

"Yeah, well I may have been up there with those hoity toity Yankees, but I know where I come from."

She laughed. "Well, I like Georgia; it's becoming my home. Connecticut is okay, and that was all I knew until dad came here for work. But I don't like Mom's husband."

"Yeah. You said that. Tell me about that."

"It's complicated," she sighed.

"I don't mind."

"Alright. Mom's a psychiatrist and she fell in love with a patient, which is usually like a huge no-no. But, he switched doctors so that they could date. Two years later, here we are."

"So, why don't you like him?" he asked.

"Because I feel like he uses her. Mom works really hard but this guy is... he's just a recovering drunk and I don't believe that he really loves my mom. He doesn't have a job and mom says he just needs 'mental time' to get back on his feet." She sighed heavily, looking to James, changing the subject. "So, what made you want to go into NASA?"

"When I was a little boy, I fell in love with astronomy and all things outer space. But as I grew older, I also developed a love for flying. I guess I just wanted to reach for the stars."

"You're so impressive," she said.

He stared at her while she watched the moon's light dance across the water for a moment before quickly slipping his phone out of his pocket and taking a picture of her without her notice. Then he said, "Melanie?"

Without looking up to him, she answered, "Yeah?"

"Can I kiss you?"

Considering the hesitation Amber had about her leaving with him tonight, Melanie replied, "No."

"Well I don't like *that*," he said, feeling rejected but also disappointed.

She glanced discreetly over to him, noticing his disappointment, reconsidering her statement.

"James?"

He looked to her, hopeful that she'd rethought her decision. "Is that a 'yes'?" he asked.

"Yes."

He moved in closer, gently holding her face in his hands, planting their lips together. Melanie returned the kiss ardently, wrapping her arms around him, firmly gripping ahold of his shirt with one hand, and weaving her fingers into his soft hair with her other. She parted her lips just slightly to allow his tongue access to hers, and she inhaled slightly as he began to stroke her tongue with his. He pulled her over to his lap, straddling her legs to either side of his, maneuvering his hands under the edge of the t-shirt in order to feel the skin of her shoulder blades. She jumped slightly at his touch, surprised at his advances, but was eager and willing, and allowed his wandering hands access to a few inches underneath her shirt, until his hands started venturing forward, trying to get a better feel. Then she whispered, "Those aren't for you yet." But she wanted more and resumed kissing, and he let out a frustrated sigh and moved his lips to her earlobe and her jawline, holding her face in his hands as he kissed, whispering, "Throw a guy a bone." Then he moved his hands to her backside, pulling her hips closer to his as he allowed his passion to overwhelm him, and his hands moved all the way up the back of her t-shirt to the neckline.

Their kissing continued like this for many minutes, until Melanie began to hear his moans of pleasure and felt his fingers begin to tease the waistline of her jeans, slipping a few fingers in-between her pants and skin to begin the search for her panty line, and the other hand maneuvered down onto her backside as he started lifting her up, tilting to lay her back. She pulled away.

"Wait," she said.

"I apologize," he replied, thinking he was moving too quickly.

"Let's go somewhere else," she suggested.

His eyes lit up as he quickly stood, holding out his hand to help her stand.

"I live with my family when I'm here. I'm with Willis in Connecticut, but..."

"Well, I live with my dad, obviously," she replied.

"Yeah... that doesn't work," he hesitated.

"It's okay. Just take me wherever you're comfortable."

"We'll go to my place. No one will know. They don't bother me," he said, leading her back to the truck.

TWO

Melanie woke up in James's bed and was a mixture of emotions ranging from sheer bliss to piercing worry.

"James." She shook him, trying to wake him as he snored next to her. "James." She tried once more. But watching him sleep, she found herself admiring his messy blonde hair and slim, pink lips, with the bottom lip just fuller than the top, and his long, pointed nose that dropped perfectly to accent those beautiful lips. Her mind was intoxicated by his muscular physique that pushed her beyond her limits during her first time ever having sex last night.

"Melanie," he said as he kissed all over her. "You are the most beautiful woman I have ever seen. I think I'm in love with you."

She giggled and tried to cover herself, but he moved her hands and resumed kissing all down the front of her.

"Don't cover those. I need more time here," he mumbled as he kissed.

"But you make me feel so shy!"

"Don't be shy," he said and paused to look up to her face. "I'm captivated by you. I need more of you." And he disappeared under the covers once more, resuming his kissing, as she squirmed and tugged on his hair from the way his lips were tickling her ribs...

But her thoughts about their love session was soon interrupted with a strong pound on the door.

"James!" Amber banged. "James!!!"

"*Shit,*" he grumbled, rubbing his eyes and sitting up. He looked to Melanie and kissed her cheek, whispering, "Good morning, gorgeous girl. I could get used to waking up next to this pretty face. Did you sleep alright?"

"Yes." She nodded. But then Amber angrily pounded again.

"James Tyler! I know something is going on. Now answer this door!"

"Ugh. Sisters," he groaned. Then he stood, threw on his boxers, and walked to open the door, where Amber was waiting to lecture him.

"Did ya get my friend home alright last night?"

"What?" he responded, yawning and stretching where he stood in the doorway, and Melanie secretly admired him from where she laid on his bed, peeking out from under his blanket.

"I know you didn't because her dad called here asking to talk to her, since she wasn't answering her cell. And don't answer the door in only your boxers anymore; it's disgusting. Where is she?" Amber forced the door open looking for Melanie, who was clearly hiding under his covers.

James shrugged and let out a sigh of dismissal. But Amber knew better and looked to the human figure under the tan blanket.

"That's her. Isn't it, James!?!" she yelled angrier than Melanie had ever heard from her before, and she walked inside his room. "Melanie! I know it's you! Did you sleep with James last night?!" She pulled down the covers to reveal Melanie's reddening face.

"Hi, Ambs," Melanie waved, knowing that she had some explaining to do with her best friend.

"Ew! Gross!!! What *were* you thinking?!" Amber reproved. Then she looked to James, "And *you*! How could you?! She's my *best* friend! I told you to keep your peter in your pants!"

"Oh, Amber. Shut it and *get* out!" He grabbed her arm, yanking her toward the door.

"I am *so* not letting this go! I can't believe you did this! What about what's-her-face redhead?" Amber added, as he pushed her face through the door and slammed it closed.

Then he walked back over to his bed where Melanie was now sitting up wearing the t-shirt he'd given her to wear last night.

"Feel free to keep that shirt..." he began, but she interrupted.

"Who was Amber talking about?" she asked.

"Who's that?"

"She referred to her as 'redhead what's-her-face'. You know what I mean. Do you have a girlfriend? Am I a one night stand?! Oh no, even *worse*. Am I the '*other woman*'?!" She yelled, grabbing a pillow and angrily pounding him with it, repeatedly.

"Melanie! Please," he begged as he was being clobbered with the pillow.

"You're a pig! You think because you are some Ivy League smarty pants that you can come here and take advantage of an inexperienced virgin, who'd never even kissed a man in her life before you!" she yelled.

"What?" he said.

"Yeah, James. Not only have I never had sex before, you're my first kiss too," she said.

"I didn't... know... Melanie," he stuttered, as she pounded him a few more times, and he watched her slip on her pants and walk out.

He collapsed back onto the bed to get lost in his thoughts for a few minutes before Amber came busting back in.

"Happy with yourself?"

"Lay off it. Would you Amber? I didn't know she was *so* inexperienced. She is *your* friend after all."

"Well, you're heading back to school tomorrow and you aren't continuing *whatever* this is. Understand? I don't want you playing your games with my friends!"

"I'm coming back for the summer," he said, with a smirk and a shrug.

"No," Amber said before slamming the door closed behind herself.

NEW HAVEN

"James, buddy. Why aren't you talking to any girls tonight? None of them meeting your *low* standards?" Willis laughed and motioned for the bartender to give him another beer.

"Nah." He sighed. "I've just got my mind on something else is all."

"What is it?" Willis asked, turning around to see that James hadn't even touched his first whiskey sour but had been looking through pictures on his phone instead. "What the hell are you doing, man?"

"Nothing. Just feeling stressed," he said.

"It's a girl. I know it is. *All* these years of girl hopping and my best friend has *finally* found *the one*. I can tell. You're like a brother to me and I know when it's more than lust. I know because it's only ever been lust until this moment right now. James is finally in love! Who is it? C'mon, lover. Tell me," Willis teased, half-drunk, as James stared at the picture on his phone of Melanie sitting on the bridge.

"I'm not doing this. We aren't having this discussion. I'm not in love."

"Right. And the Pope ain't Catholic neither. Just tell me who it is! I can help you out, man. Unless... *Shit.* It's Amber's friend that you..." He reached for James's phone and saw that he was right. "Holy hell. Amber's gon' kill you! You know that don't you?!" Willis laughed and slapped James on the back as he hung his head in his hand. "That's all right. I got your back. We leave Connecticut to go back to Atlanta next week. You've got the whole summer, man."

GRADUATION

"Can you believe it?!" Amber exclaimed as they put on their caps and gowns and prepared themselves for graduation.

"Yep. It's exciting," Melanie replied.

"Mel? What's wrong? What's with you this week? You're not yourself," Amber said.

Melanie's eyes filled with tears and spilled over, not ready to tell her best friend her deepest secret.

"I have something that I need to tell you, but you have to promise not to freak out on me. Okay?"

"Of course I won't. I swear."

Melanie inhaled deeply and said, "I'm late."

"You mean?"

Melanie nodded. "I've only been with *one* guy."

"Oh *god*," Amber groaned. "You can't be serious. Why does this shit always happen to *me*?! I have enough drama in my crazy family already. Now to involve you in it! Ugh!!!"

"You promised you weren't going to freak out!"

"Didn't he use protection?" Amber asked.

"Kind of?" Melanie shrugged.

"Kind of? What does that even mean? Never mind. I don't want to know. I'm just going to kill him!" Amber shouted.

"What's he going to say? You know him best," Melanie asked.

"I don't know. I mean, he's not really a *girlfriend* type." Amber shook her head looking out to the crowd of people in the hallway.

"But you said..." Melanie began as they exited the school bathroom and gathered in with the other students. She opened the auditorium doors and peered out to the thousands of people, noticing her mom and dad in the audience, though not seated together. But she also saw Amber's family, James included (who she thought looked incredibly handsome with his blonde hair combed back, and in his well-fitted black pants and long-sleeved blue shirt with the sleeves rolled up to his elbows). She wanted to smile at the sight but couldn't because she was 99% certain she was pregnant and with *his* baby.

" *What* did I say?" Amber asked.

Melanie turned from her ogling and replied, "When you saw me in his room, you said that he had some redheaded what's-her-face. I thought you meant he had a girlfriend, which is why I stormed out that morning."

"Oh god, no. Nothing like that. He kept a poster of *I Love Lucy* on his wall as a teenager and everyone made fun of him for it. Now it's hanging in his college dorm because it's still like his favorite show ever, and he's got this obsession with redheads, like every girl he's ever brought home has had red hair, until you. There's still a poster in his bedroom too. Didn't you notice it? We told him if he ever found a woman she'd make him get rid of that stupid poster. He's such a loser!" Amber said with a laugh, rolling her eyes.

"I suppose I wasn't focused on the *things* in his room," Melanie said, and Amber let out a disgusted sigh.

Melanie cracked open the doors to peek out to the crowd of people once again, this time with a small smile on her face, but still wondering how she was ever going to tell him.

"Miss Melanie Ann Crosby," the superintendent called out, as Melanie walked across the auditorium stage to take her diploma. She shook his hand and looked to the audience, taking notice of her dad and mom standing. Then she glanced to the left of them, where she saw James's head cradled heavily in his hands and his elbows were rocking on his knees. She quickly looked away, understanding that she truly was a one-night stand.

"We did it!!!" Amber exclaimed as they met each other in the foyer to toss their caps with the rest of the graduating class.

Melanie spread her arms out wide and embraced Amber while the rest of the class surrounded them.

They removed their blue caps, yelled, "2013!" and tossed them into the air.

Melanie and Amber walked to the parking lot to leave and Amber asked if Melanie would be attending her graduation party that evening. But Melanie hesitated, mostly because she knew that James was going to be hanging around. Amber tried to reassure her that James would be distracted by his cousins and other family members present, but Melanie was still worried about how she was going to face him, feeling certain that she was nothing more than a whim of fancy to him, something he looked at, liked, and went for, but then forgot about. Now she was in complete understanding why Amber had warned her about him, and she was feeling regretful over not heeding her friend's caution. Pregnant at 18? How would she ever manage?

After saying goodbye to a few friends, she waved to Amber and found her dad.

"Please come tonight!" Amber yelled, as Melanie got into her dad's car.

"Is your friend coming to your party?" James asked Amber while they walked toward his truck together.

"Maybe. But don't be getting any ideas. Stay away from her."

"Who are you to dictate what I can and can't do? I can't stop thinking about her. This past month all I've wanted to do was see her again, Amber. I wanted to call and talk to her. I like spending time with her."

"Hold up. Wait." Amber stopped where she stood and turned to face him before continuing. "Is this James— the man who claims he's never going to be tied down to anyone in his entire life— admitting that he's actually *interested* in someone? I don't believe it. She's my best friend and I don't want you to hurt her. Just tell me. Are you really serious? No games?"

"Possibly. I don't know yet. I only went out with her once. But I'm admitting that I'd like to *maybe* see where it goes."

"Hm... well my bets are that she would too," Amber sassed.

"You know this for sure?" he asked.

"No. But, just trust me on this."

That evening at the party, Melanie showed up in a stunning, white summer dress in order to make James realize what he was missing out on, determined to make him regret not contacting her at all since that night he took advantage of her innocence.

"Hey, Mel!" Amber hollered, as she walked into the great room in the Hunters' big, expensive house. Their father, Bruce, was a pilot for a major airline and their mother, Janice, was a lawyer for a big firm, placing the Hunters on the higher end of the wealthy spectrum.

Janice and Bruce were typical southerners, friendly, inviting, and relaxed. Janice's looks and demeanor were sociable, yet fit for her status in society, as she was always dressed in a semi-business casual look, and her blonde, modern voluminous shag was never out of place, always fixed to perfection, teased with just the right amount of southern love.

But the kids got their height from Bruce, at 6 feet tall, a lanky man with dark hair, the girls tended to take their features from him rather than their mother. While James, though tall, his blonde hair and blue eyes were attributed to his mother.

"Hi, Amber!" Melanie waved as she put her purse on the coat rack and walked into the living room, trying to maneuver herself through the crowd of people.

"Just relax and breathe. James is in the den getting drunk with some of my cousins. We will make our appearance out here, but we'll go downstairs with our friends and hang. He won't bother us down there," she reassured.

Melanie nodded but asked, "Do you have food? I'm starving."

Laughter erupted from Amber before she whispered, "Okay, preggers."

"Who's pregnant?" James asked as he peeked out from around the corner next to Amber, holding a beer in his hand and finishing off a few chips.

"Oh my god, Mel. I'm so sorry," Amber mouthed.

"What's wrong?" he asked. "What'd I miss?"

"Number one... *you* are half wasted, so you need to stop talking. Number two... you need to take this one and go upstairs." And she motioned for Melanie to take him upstairs.

"Do we need to talk?" he asked.

Melanie just nodded, so he grabbed her arm and pulled her along, up and into his room.

After closing and locking his bedroom door behind him, he turned to face her, when he noticed tears streaming down her face.

"Melanie? Are you angry at me? My sister is wrong. I've only had like three beers. I'm not wasted. I just like to mess around with her," he said.

"Why didn't you call me?" she asked.

"Um," he replied, scrunching half his face, unsure of what to say.

"We have nothing to talk about. I better go." She stood to leave, but he quickly reached for her arm.

"Wait. What did you want to tell me?"

"I'm pregnant," she blurted out, plopping down onto the bed, hiding her worried face in her hands.

"Well, hell," he mumbled, running his hands over his face, as he sat down next to her.

"I don't expect anything from you. You didn't call me for a reason. I'm sorry I even told you," she sniffled.

"Hey," he moved her hands, trying to get her to look at him, saying, "I'm not upset, just surprised, I suppose. But I think I can make this work. Hey, don't cry."

Inhaling deeply, frustrated that he still hadn't admitted to why he never called, she stood to leave once more. "You never called."

"Melanie, I didn't call you because my sister asked me not to. I thought I was doing a good thing. Though you weren't my first, you've been my most *memorable*."

"A girl never forgets her first kiss, which might be more important than the first time she has sex. I've thought about you every day, James." She turned toward the door and reached for the knob just as he hollered for her once more.

"Melanie! Believe me, I thought about you every day too. Look..." He stood and walked over to her and showed her the

33

picture of her on his phone that he'd secretly taken while they were sitting on the bridge together.

"I looked at it every day," he said. Then he took her face in his hands and kissed her passionately.

"So, what now?" she asked, pulling away from his kiss, dropping her face to stare at his beige carpet.

"I guess we have a baby." He pulled her face up to kiss him once more, but she pulled away again to ask, "No. I mean about *us.*"

"Oh. Well, I would assume that this means you're my girlfriend. If you want to be..."

Again, he resumed his kissing, but this time lifting her up, carrying her over to the bed, gently dropping her down. When their lips parted, she said, "Well, I actually was wondering how it's going to work."

In between kisses, he said, "Do you mean... because I'm there... and you're here?"

"Mmmhm," she agreed as she reached up under his shirt to feel the bulging ridges of his abdominal muscles, and he began unzipping the back of her dress, laying her back.

"Well, I have my own place on campus. Well, me and Willis, and you *could* come there," he suggested.

"Are you *that* serious about me? You didn't even want me to be your girlfriend until you found out I was pregnant with your child. You didn't even watch me walk across the stage at my graduation." She sat up and zipped her dress.

"What?" he asked.

"I looked down to you as I received my diploma this afternoon, and you weren't even watching. You were staring at the floor."

He sat up next to her. "Melanie, you have *no idea* how beautiful I thought you looked today and how frustrated I was that I thought I couldn't act on it because of Amber. She bitched to my dad about me, and he was going to pull some of my funding unless I stayed away from you because she convinced him that I tricked you into going out with me."

"Oh. So, you would've called?" she asked, lightly taking his fingers in hers.

"You're damn right I would've, had it not been for Amber's meddling."

Melanie sighed and laid back down, pulling on his shirt to pull him down next to her, then playing with his hair. "So where does that leave us then?"

"Well, we are having a baby and..."

"I'm coming to Connecticut with you?" she asked, as he kissed around her neck.

"You bet your ass you are."

THREE

"Did you want to take your own things so it feels more like home?" Melanie's dad, Greg, asked while he helped pack her things from her room.

"No. I'll have furniture. Besides, I'm going to need this stuff for when I come and visit. I'm only going to take essentials. Hey, Dad?"

"Yeah, sugar?"

"Thanks for being so supportive and cool about this. I love you."

"You're welcome. I'll always be here for you. Just promise me something," he said.

"Anything."

Greg walked over, hugging her, "Promise me that you won't let whatever happens with this guy break your beautiful spirit. Okay?"

"I promise," she agreed.

"I have something for you. Here. Take this." He handed her a credit card and keys. "There's some money in a bank account I opened for you. And I don't want you relying on him for everything, so there's a car in my garage for you when you need it. I love you, sugar. I'm always here for you," he said.

"I love you too. Thanks Dad." She hugged him before he took her bags and headed to the front door.

"Ready?" James asked from the front porch where he'd been waiting to load her bags into his truck.

Melanie nodded and looked to her dad, as James reached to take Melanie's bags, but Greg set them down instead.

"James," Greg said, looking to Melanie.

"Go ahead on to the truck, Melanie. I'll be right there," James said, knowing Greg wanted to talk. "Mr. Crosby?" James asked, when he saw that Melanie was nearer to the truck.

James was never intimidated by Melanie's dad because his stocky 5'11" frame and 240 pounds, middle-aged, balding, dad-bod definitely wouldn't hold up to the edge James had on him with his own 6'2" muscular frame, that made him seem bulkier than the 190 pounds he actually carried. But Greg's protective attitude of Melanie did give James an awareness to be on alert.

"I'm going to put it real to you, young man. Not only is she my only daughter, she's also my only child and that makes this a pretty sticky situation for you. I'm a pretty open individual and I know we're not living in the dark ages, so I'm trying to be cool about all of this. Now, I know my daughter is a beautiful girl and she's had offers from guys before, which she's turned down. I don't know what she sees in you that caused her attentions to shift so suddenly, but you got my daughter pregnant the first time you took her out and then you ignored her for an entire month, and now you want me to believe that you're just going to magically do right by her?"

"I..." James shrugged, brushing Greg's comment off.

"Listen here, you arrogant little shit, this is your only warning. If I believe for even one second that you're playing games with her, or messing around with other women, which I've heard from numerous sources seems to be your usual scene, then I will personally see to it that not only will your expensive rich boy's truck out there no longer be drivable, but I will also be sure that every woman in this town and in nearby vicinities knows that 'James Tyler Hunter' gets the Viagra he needs from *my* pharmacy."

"You wouldn't dare."

"Test me and find out. I don't mess around. I believe *my* daughter is waiting," Greg said and pointed to the driveway.

James picked up Melanie's bags and walked to his truck, fuming over the confrontation.

"Melanie," he said as he climbed in on his side, starting the engine, glancing back at Greg still standing in the doorway. "What have you discussed with your dad about me?"

Looking puzzled, she replied, "I'm not sure I know what you mean."

"Nothing," he said. "Never mind."

"Tell me what it is, James."

"He seems to have this idea that I'm not interested in a relationship with you. Why would he believe that?"

"Oh. Well, I might've insinuated it," she said.

"How so?" he asked.

"Um, he asked when we were going to get married and I said we aren't," she said, turning to look out the window.

"I see. *Do you* want to get married, Melanie?" he asked.

"You mean to *you*, or like *ever*?"

"To me."

"No," she said.

"Huh. Then that's that. I'm just gonna be your baby daddy." He smiled at her. Melanie smiled back, but she still felt unsure of being pregnant at 18, especially to a man she hardly knew and one that didn't love her.

When they arrived at James's house, Amber greeted her happily and Janice quickly ushered him to the spare bedroom with Melanie's things.

"Melanie! I can't believe you're going to be living here! Isn't it great?!" Amber exclaimed.

"It's great," Melanie said with as much enthusiasm as she could muster for Amber's benefit only.

"Take her bags to the spare bedroom across the hall from you. I already made it up for her," Janice said. "She needs her own space."

"She doesn't want to stay in there. Do you want to stay in there or do you want to stay with me?" he asked.

"Um, I'd like my own room," Melanie said.

"Alright, then," he said, feeling rejected.

"Mom, do you really think James has it in himself to hold down a relationship?" Amber asked, as James walked up the stairs with Melanie.

"I haven't the slightest clue. But, let's hope so," Janice replied.

"My room is bigger, Melanie. Are you sure?" James asked once they were upstairs.

"I'm sure."

"Okay. Here are your bags. Make yourself at home." He laid her bags on the bed and walked to the door, but he turned and said just before exiting, "I'm sorry I'm not what you were hoping for. If you'd like to have dinner tonight, Willis, Kaylee, and I usually go to the bar on Fridays. You can bring Amber, if you'd like. Think about it."

She closed the door behind him and started unpacking her things, burying her sadness deep inside her heart as she worked on hanging her clothes. But she thought about his words, *I'm sorry I'm not what you were hoping for,* and wanted to tell him he had not a clue, not one at all, because he was everything she wanted.

"Mel?" Amber knocked a little while later.

"Come in," she answered.

"Hey! How's it going? Getting settled?" Amber bounced over to sit on the bed.

"Yep," she shrugged, motioning to her things that were nearly put away.

"Well, good! Cause we're going out! Get dressed."

"I don't know if I have anything other than sweats to wear. My clothes are getting snug," Melanie said.

"Just pick anything," Amber said. "Jamie doesn't care what you wear."

Melanie picked out something that wasn't her usual partying scene clothes— a comfy, stretchy, summer dress. Her waistline was beginning to expand as was her chest, thus the search for suitable clothing began.

The bar was its usual Friday night action— rednecks consuming food and liquor, causing a commotion— and James, Amber, and Melanie sat at a long table to wait for Kaylee and Willis, and a waitress came up to take orders.

"Hi, ya'll. Anything to drink?" she asked.

"Whiskey sour. No cherry," James answered.

"You always get the same thing, James. Ever think of trying something new?" she asked.

He shook his head, looking away from her, glancing around the room, leaning against his chair, crossing his arms.

"How about you, honey?" she asked Melanie, who was seated by Amber, not James.

"Sweet tea, please."

"I haven't seen you around here much," the waitress said, tapping her chin, thinking, "Not since that night... Oh! You're the step dancer! We had a young gentleman in here asking to see you do that again! I need to tell him you're here!"

The mention of another man being interested in Melanie ignited a small flame of jealousy in James and he was curious about who it was that wanted to see her dance again.

A few minutes later, a man approached the table. "Hi, Melanie."

"Hi, Clay. How are you?"

"I've been doing great. Hi Amber. So, Melanie, I see that you're here with friends, but I was thinking that maybe we could hang out sometime? I mean, if you wanted." He shrugged, awaiting her response.

James clenched his jaw, narrowing his eyes at the dweeby little guy asking out his supposed new girlfriend, and he was curious what Melanie's response would be.

"That's very kind of you, but um, actually, I have a boyfriend." She pointed across the table to James, whose eyes smiled at the declaration of her announcement of him being her boyfriend.

"Oh, I wasn't aware. Sorry, man," he held up his hands apologetically to James and began backing away from the table. "Bye Melanie. Bye Amber."

Melanie waved and looked to James, who was smirking victoriously.

"What are you smiling about?" Melanie asked, as Kaylee and Willis walked up.

"Sweet satisfaction," James answered, "It's a man thing. You wouldn't understand."

"Hey guys!" Kaylee hollered out.

"Where's the food?" Willis asked. "I come to the bar where James has been sitting for a while before me and all I see is one damn whiskey sour? What kind of a messed-up world is this?" he joked.

"Well, I didn't have the chance to order food because someone was hitting on Melanie," James complained, downing his whiskey.

"Where is he? I'll mess him up!" Willis half-joked, half-threatened.

"Guys, it's not like I was interested in him. Besides, James and I are..."

"*What?*" Amber asked, leaning forward on her elbows, knowing Melanie was about to say something sassy.

"Nothing. Never mind. Let's just get some food," Melanie replied.

"The guy was from our school. He likes Melanie because of her epic dancing skills," Amber added. "Jamie, are you feeling a little bit jealous?"

He just moved his eyes to look her way while his chin rested on his hands, as his elbows seemed to be digging into the table from his range of emotions at the group's conversation, but he didn't respond.

"He doesn't have a reason to be jealous. I mean, it's not like we're serious or anything. We are only having a baby together, and though I don't intend on going out on any other dates, we've only known each other but two months," Melanie added, trying to make James feel better, but only making him think that she didn't want him.

"James, seems like you've got some work to do with this one," Willis joked. "I didn't know you were just a baby daddy." He laughed some more.

"Shut up," James snapped.

"I didn't mean it like that," Melanie said.

"Well, he's either your boyfriend or he's your baby daddy. Which is it?" Kaylee asked.

Melanie looked across the table to James, admiring how handsome she thought he was, remembering the passionate night they'd spent together and thought about how much she wanted a repeat of that, and replied, "He's my boyfriend."

"How does that suit you, Jamie?" Amber asked. "You've never had a girlfriend. Are you ready for commitment?"

He looked at Melanie's pretty brown eyes as they stared directly into his, and he imagined having a sweet little girl looking just like her, so he replied, "Yeah. I'm good."

Later that evening upon returning home, James had just finished showering and was walking down the hallway to his bedroom, when he noticed Melanie's bedroom door wasn't latched but her light was off.

"Melanie?" he whispered, cracking the door to look inside, noticing her lying on the bed in just his t-shirt and her underwear. Quietly, he tip-toed over to cover her with the blanket.

"Goodnight," he whispered, brushing the hair away from her face and kissing her forehead.

"Goodnight," she whispered back.

"Oh. I didn't realize you were awake."

She patted the bed for him to lay with her, which he did willingly, and he lifted the blankets and crawled underneath, covering them up, cuddling her in his arms.

"Were you jealous of my friend from school tonight?" she asked.

"Yes," he answered.

"Why?"

"I don't know. There's something about you that's stirring an emotional discord in me and I was worried that you wouldn't feel strongly enough about what we have going on to make us exclusive."

"So... are *you* only considering us exclusive from this point on?" she asked, pulling away from his embrace.

"No! NO... that's not what I meant. What I *meant* was that I know you're so beautiful, and men are going to hit on you all the time. But I'm such a screw up and I'm going to continually disappoint you. I know you're going to have the opportunity to go elsewhere, but I'm hoping that you won't. I'm hoping that you'll stay, you know, with *me*."

"James, don't be afraid of commitment." She wrapped her arms up around his neck, pulling him in for a kiss.

"Hey," he asked a few minutes later, when his kisses were getting more passionate.

"Yeah?"

"You know, I have a bigger room..." he continued kissing, pulling the Bulldogs shirt up over her head, and he moved his kisses lower, "and..." he said, continuing his kisses as they trailed down her chest, where he paused for a moment, causing giggling to erupt from her, but also for Amber to bang on the wall, yelling, "I can hear you! Stop whatever it is you're doing in there!"

James looked up, irritated, and slightly shifted his body so he could pound back. "NO! Turn on your TV and ignore us! Get a life, loser!"

She yelled back immediately, "You're the one who has to get with *my* friends!!"

"Okay. Your room it is," Melanie said, rolling out from underneath him, throwing on the t-shirt. "We'll move my things in tomorrow."

"It's a good decision anyway. My grandparents sleep in here." He winked.

Melanie laughed, as he grabbed her hand, pulling her across the hall, closing and locking the door behind them.

"Where were we?" he asked, pulling off her t-shirt, sitting down on his bed.

She straddled his lap, resuming, but pulled away to ask, "Had the situation been in reverse tonight, would you have turned down an invitation to dinner?"

"Yes," he said.

"How do I know?" she asked.

"Because I'm here with you, kissing all over you, waiting for you to stop asking ridiculous questions and let me have you." He switched positions and put her down on the bed, hovering over her, holding her head in his hands, "And I'm not still at the bar waiting for a girl, like I normally would be."

She leaned up on her elbows. "Was that your usual scene? Is that how you picked me?"

"Melanie..."

"I'm sorry," she took his face in her hands, returning his kissing. "You know, we have to discuss this eventually."

"What?" he asked while she worked on removing his shirt, running her hand down the ridges of his muscles, until she reached his boxers, touching her fingers along the edge.

"Our pasts. I mean, you know mine. But I need to know yours," she shrugged.

"Okay," he agreed. "But not right now," he said, moving his lips to her collar bone, rubbing his hands on the curve of her hips to tease his fingers underneath her panty line and slowly maneuver them downward.

"Eventually," she sighed, giving in to him as he moved his mouth to her bellybutton and down...

FOUR

"You see that bright spot right there?" the sonographer pointed to the monitor.

Melanie nodded and looked to James, who only shrugged, and she was certain that he was the most confused genius she'd ever met.

The sonographer smiled and continued, "Well, that's your baby. You're 10 weeks and 6 days along. Congratulations. This is the heartbeat..."

His smile curled up ever-so-slightly listening to the steady whooping sound of the baby's heartbeat.

"When will we know if it's a boy or a girl?" he asked.

"About 20 weeks or so," the tech responded.

"Do you want to find out?" Melanie looked to him, taking his hand.

"If you do," he nodded.

She nodded too, happy that he was engaging with her in this.

The tech printed some pictures for them to keep and Melanie admired them the whole ride home, while James tried his hardest to figure out what he was looking at.

"It just looks like a blob to me, but I think it's the most beautiful blob I've ever seen. How are you feeling?"

"My stomach kind of aches. I'm ready for a nap," she replied.

"We can do that. I like naps," he said, "Especially with you."

"Are you happy?" she asked, just as they neared the house.

"Do you mean about the baby?" he asked.

"Yes."

"I'm happy, Melanie. I'm happy about the baby, you, about everything. There's nothing else I want."

"Okay." She smiled, her heart feeling satisfied.

They pulled into the driveway and saw Janice and Amber waiting at the doorway.

"Prepare yourself," he said, helping her down from the truck. "Mom is going to want to keep the pictures. Don't let her. They're ours."

"Heh. Right, then you take them. Guard them with your life," she said, handing them to him. But he refused.

"No way. She has leverage on me. It's your job," he replied just as they walked inside and Janice approached them.

"Let's see them!" Janice exclaimed happily as they walked in and Melanie set her purse down on the entryway table.

Melanie handed her the pictures of the baby and Janice squealed in excitement.

"I want you to know that you will want for nothing. Understand?" she kissed Melanie's cheek, hugging her. "But you, young man," she turned to James, "This is a good girl. You better do right by her!"

"He already knocked her up. What else can he screw up?" Amber said.

"Shut up, Amber!" James retorted.

"Great come back, Jamie."

"Are you sure you don't want to stay here the year while he finishes school? You could have his room, or you can just have the spare. I want to be around for that little one and then you wouldn't have to be alone," Janice asked.

"She won't *be* alone, Mom. I'll be there. Also, her mom lives nearby. It's out of the question. I want her with me," James responded.

"Jamie, but you'll be so busy with classes," Janice tried convincing.

"It's not up for discussion," he refused.

"Mom, you know when Jamie gets something into his head," Amber chimed in again.

"I know..." she sighed, as he walked away from them and upstairs to his room with Melanie.

"I'm really sleepy and I'm not feeling very well," she said holding her tummy, gesturing that she felt sick. "I'm going to lie down."

"That's fine. Why don't you get changed? Here..." he said, tossing her a pair of sweats, while he watched her strip down to only her bra and underwear. "I really want you there with me," he said, "My mom doesn't know what life is like for me at school. I have a lot of time in between classes and I can help. I swear I will."

"Jamie, what do you see for us? Like what's in our future? You haven't known me very long. Do you love me?" she asked, as she slipped into his sweats.

He thought on her question for a minute before he said, "Oh... um... I guess I never thought about love before now but..."

"Ow..." she cried out and hunched over, clutching her stomach.

"What is it?" he asked, hurrying to her side, helping her up to sit on the bed.

"Nothing. I'm okay. But my stomach feels like I'm going to throw up and I'm having this terrible ache in my side," she said, pointing to her lower right side.

"Well, why don't you lie down for a bit? You need as much rest as you can get," he said, helping her move to lay back. But as soon as she went to move, she cried out again, buckling to her knees, hunching over, grasping at her stomach, letting a few tears fall.

"Oh! Ow!" she said.

"You're not okay. Come here... I think you should go see someone." He knelt down and lifted her up. She wrapped her arms around his neck, resting her head against his chest as he carefully carried her down the stairs.

"Amber!" he called.

"What..." Amber complained, until she walked into the great room and saw Melanie draped over his arms, tears soaking her cheeks, dripping off her chin onto his t-shirt. "I'll get your truck," Amber replied, correcting her attitude and offering.

"What's hurting?" he asked.

"I have this terrible ache in my lower abdomen." She placed both hands on her tummy to the right of her belly button, scrunching her face. "Right here," she said. "Jamie? I'm scared."

He sighed and said, "It's going to be okay," and then he kissed her earlobe to give her some comfort. But his heart was in mayhem, worried for her and their baby.

Amber had his truck pulled to the front of the large house where the circular driveway met at the door, and Janice hurried to open it as he approached.

"I'll meet you there," Janice said as James laid Melanie inside on the backseat of his truck.

"Call me when you get there," he said, walking to his side and hurrying to climb in. Amber quickly joined him, climbing in the front passenger seat.

"Jamie," Melanie said, sitting up about five minutes away from the ER.

As he looked back to her, she held her stomach, placed her hand over her mouth, and dry heaved a few times before vomiting all over the back of his beautiful leather seats.

Amber winced at the sight, looking to James, knowing how particular he was about his expensive truck, and she watched him sigh and run his fingers through his hair, then faced forward, not saying anything to Melanie but focusing his frustrations on driving instead.

Upon arrival, Amber rushed inside to get her a wheelchair, alerting the triage nurse.

James helped Melanie down out of the truck, despite the vomit that was on her. However, she still felt nervous about making such a mess because he hadn't declared intimate feelings for her and she felt it possible that he was only doing the noble and honorable thing by her because that was in his character, but not because he loved or wanted her.

"I'm so sorry," she apologized as he was helping her into the wheelchair to take her inside.

"Don't worry about it. I'll take it to the detailer later," he brushed it off.

"Your face says something else, James."

"What do you mean?" he asked.

"Just forget it."

The nurse measured her vitals and took her medical history. "Who is your medical decision maker?" she asked.

"Excuse me?" Melanie replied.

"Well, if something serious were to happen and we needed someone to make decisions for you, then who were that to be?" the nurse continued.

"Oh. Well, my mom lives in Connecticut..." she began, so the nurse interrupted.

"Who lives nearby?"

"My dad."

"We'll put him down. Name please?" the nurse asked.

"Greg Crosby."

In that moment, James realized that he didn't like how someone else was going to be deciding Melanie's future, suddenly feeling very afraid for her.

The nurse handed her a gown to change and prepped her for an IV to give her some pain meds.

"I'll be in the hall," James said as he walked out.

"Jamie?" Melanie called after him.

"He's probably just stressed," Amber said. "He doesn't handle emotional situations well. Never has."

"Oh. I think I freaked him out today," Melanie said as she stood to put the gown on.

"Why? What happened?" Amber asked, turning around to give Melanie privacy.

"Well, just before all of this went down, we were having a conversation about me moving with him and... Oh! Ow!" she cried out in pain, crouching down, holding her stomach.

The nurse hurried over, steadying her, and pulling her onto the bed, adjusting her gown. "I'll get the doctor right away," she said, giving her the shot of pain meds in her IV. "Shouldn't be too long." The nurse walked out.

Melanie's tears came harder now from the unyielding pain, but mostly because she was fretting over James. She knew he didn't love her and she didn't want to be stuck in a relationship where the guy felt forced to be with someone because of a pregnancy. The torment she felt inside her soul might've been hurting her more than the pain she felt inside her tummy.

A technician came in a short while later to take Melanie for some testing, and Janice showed up while she was gone.

"Where's Melanie?" Janice asked Amber and James, who had returned to the room while Melanie was out for testing.

"She's having a scan," Amber replied.

"Okay. Do they think it's the baby?" Janice asked.

Amber shrugged.

"James, you're awfully quiet and I think it's scaring Melanie. You need to bring this girl some sort of comfort," Amber said.

"Lay off it, Amber," James retorted.

"Really. What's with you? Melanie has got to be scared out of her mind and all you can seem to do is sit there," she continued, while she glanced out to the hallway to watch for Melanie's return.

"This is all new to me, Amber. Haven't you considered that I might be just as nervous? Can you just give me a break once in a while?" he said as he paced back and in forth inside the room, anxiously awaiting Melanie's return.

The doctor walked in just then, with Melanie not in sight.

"Melanie is being taken immediately to surgery," he explained.

James turned to face him, wanting more information. "Why? What's wrong?" he asked.

"Her appendix is ruptured. We have to remove it immediately to prevent further complications and to avoid the loss of your baby," the doctor explained further.

"How serious is this?" James asked.

"Very. There's a high likelihood for her to develop a dangerous infection. We need to act quickly." The doctor walked out and James dropped himself into the chair behind where he stood, while Janice started gathering up all their things. Then James looked up to her, teary-eyed, surprising his mom.

"James?" she asked.

"She thinks I don't love her."

Janice stopped what she was doing and walked over to him, placing her hand on his shoulder.

"Whatever is going on between you two I'm sure will be worked out," Janice reassured with a hug.

"Not if she's dead."

He stood and followed the nurse, who escorted them to the surgical waiting area, where James paced the length of the room for two hours, while Greg drank coffee after coffee between phone calls to Melanie's mother, Lori, in Connecticut.

Finally, the surgeon emerged.

"She's in recovery and two of you can go see her now. But..."

"But what?" James interrupted.

Greg looked to James, urging him to relax and allow the doctor to speak. "What is it?"

"Her body took on a lot of the infection and we aren't sure how the pregnancy will react. There is a stable heart beat from the fetus currently; however, it's too soon to tell. We have her on a steady dose of strong antibiotics to fight the infection, but the body's ability to guard the fetus in utero will shield the baby from that protection. However, that's a good thing too, because it should also guard the baby from the infection, we hope."

James sank down into a nearby chair at the doctor's words and dropped his face into his hands as he rested his elbows distraughtly on his knees and motioned for his mother to accompany Greg in to see Melanie, while he sat... just that way.

"Melanie?" Janice said as they approached her bedside.

"Hi, sugar," Greg said, taking his daughter's hand. "How are you feeling?"

Melanie opened her eyes expecting to see James standing there and her breath escaped her and tears pricked her eyes when she saw that he was not.

"Hi Daddy. Hi Janice." She sank her head back into the pillow trying not to show her distress over wishing to see James instead.

"What's the matter sweetie?" Janice asked.

"It's nothing. I'm uh... I'm just feeling overwhelmed at everything. That's all," she sniffled and wiped her tears.

"The doctor says the baby will most likely be okay. That's good news. Glad to see you doing okay. James is very worried for you," Janice said.

"Where is he?" she asked.

"In the lobby," Janice replied.

"Is Amber here?" Melanie asked as she watched her dad take a peek at the medication drip, and she smiled at the pharmacist nature inside him getting curious.

"Yes. I'll go get her. You rest up. We want to make sure that little peanut and his Mama are doin' just fine," Janice responded, gently hugging her before walking out.

Greg kissed her forehead and said, "I made a few calls to your Mom, but she's worried sick. Text her or call when you feel up to it. You know how she can be." Then he walked out.

Feeling despaired at the absence of James, Melanie sank further down into the hospital bed placing her hand softly over her tummy, as she whispered, "Even if he doesn't love us, I'll love you with all there is of me, until my last breath."

She sniffled once more and wiped her tears. Hearing footsteps, assuming it was Amber, she said, "Hi Amber."

"Melanie," he responded as he approached the bed and held her hand. "I know..."

"Oh," she interrupted, and maneuvered herself to sit up and motioned for him to sit next to her.

He sighed deeply and avoided what he was going to say, instead asking, "Are you in a lot of pain?"

Looking away from him, she shook her head, "No. They have me on that drip right there." She pointed to the IV pole.

"Good. I was really worried for you."

"Look," she began and looked away from him. "Maybe it's just better if..."

"If what?"

"I know you don't have strong feelings for me and that you'd intended for me to be a one-night stand. Amber said that you never planned on having a family at all."

He let out a frustrated sigh and stood, crossing his arms, facing away from her.

She continued, "I don't want to be with a man who feels pressured or obligated..."

"Stop!" he yelled.

She gasped at his reaction and looked away again, while he took a moment to calm himself before he said, "Amber doesn't know as much about me as she thinks, Melanie."

"But when I asked you..."

"Asked me what?"

"Earlier I asked if you... you know, *love* me. You didn't respond."

Unable to make that kind of commitment to her yet. Uncertain if he really *did* love her, not sure if it was truly *love* that he was feeling for her, or if it was just happiness, he didn't answer. He avoided the question.

"I was just..." he paused and walked back over to the bed, sitting next to her. "She was right when she said that I'd never *planned* on having a family. But that's because I have a lot of goals for myself, and that was before..."

"Yeah, before you knocked me up," she stated.

"No, Melanie. Before I realized I care a lot about you."

Although she was happy at that declaration, she was unsure about the lack of words, "I love you" from his mouth. Even still, she reveled in the moment.

"You do?" she asked.

He leaned forward and held her face in his hands, planting a soft kiss on her forehead, and said, "Very much. I told you I was worried for you and I meant it. I've never felt such a mixture of emotions in my entire life and I didn't know what to do with it. I was so afraid I would never see you again. I'd never felt such fear."

"Aw, guys!" Amber squealed as she walked in. "I thought you were just doin' it!"

James discreetly rolled his eyes so that only Melanie would see and she winked back, knowing that Amber was going to have a field day with their new-found romance.

"Okay. So... when's the big day?" Amber asked, flinging her arms around James where he sat on the bed to give him a big squeeze.

"What *are* you talking about?" he asked, looking undeniably annoyed.

"Well, you guys are having a baby and you just admitted that you have feelings for her. I mean, it's only natural that you *should.*"

Knowing what Amber was going to say, and not wanting to freak him out, Melanie interrupted, "Oh, Amber, we aren't thinking about anything like that. He still has a year of school left and..."

"It's my job to do the asking, not yours, Amber. Quit meddling so much," he added.

Melanie was discharged three days later, but trouble was not about to leave them yet.

FIVE

"Mel, which tie do you think looks best with this shirt?" James held up two ties to his deep blue shirt and stood in front of the long mirror that was hanging on his closet door and looked to Melanie for her approval.

"I like the silver and black one," she said, walking over to tie it for him. "I'm going to miss you this evening. Do you have to go?"

"Yeah," he groaned. "I promised my dad I would sit through the presentation with him."

"What exactly is it again?" she asked, as he turned to face her, and she tightened the tie and brushed the lint off his dress shirt with her fingers.

He turned back to the mirror, grabbing his hair product off the dresser next to him, saying "The airline he works for is having a benefit and there is a special presenter from the Air Force that is speaking on advances in jet engines and thrusts..."

She wrapped her arms around his chest and held her finger up to his lips, quieting him. "It's fine. You're confusing me, my genius. You know I don't know anything about those things. Just promise me something?"

"Sure," he answered while he continued gelling his hair.

"You won't fall for any non-pregnant stewardesses with blonde hair and bright red lipstick?"

He chuckled at her comment and moved her arms from his chest so he could turn to face her.

"You are the only woman who turns my head." He kissed her.

But she mumbled through their kiss, "What about your fiery redhead?"

"Well, you *and* Lucy," he continued kissing her.

"Will I be sharing you with Lucy forever?" she mumbled.

"She's part of this package," he said as he lifted her into his arms and carried her over to the bed, gently sitting her down on his lap, kissing her more fervently.

She moved to straddle his legs and wrapped her arms around him, saying, "Amber was right."

"Amber was right? *No.* She's never right. What'd she say?" he asked and he let his hands begin to explore under the Bulldogs t-shirt she was wearing, which had become her favorite.

"She said that you'd never give up your poster."

He smirked, moving his lips down her neck. "Well, I suppose she can be right at least once in her life. I do love it. It's not leaving."

"What would it take?" she asked. "It's so terrible, Jamie. It's not even like it's of a cover girl or something," she glanced to the side of the room to his poster of Lucy, which was from the episode of Lucy stealing chocolates from the conveyor belt.

"What? You'd rather me have posters of girls in bikinis or whatever?!" he laughed and laid her back while he trailed his lips down her tummy onto her growing bump, where he paused to inspect the scar from her surgery several weeks prior.

"No! Of course not!" she said, "It's just... I've never seen or heard of a guy your age liking *I Love Lucy* so much." She continued giggling, running her fingers through his hair as he kissed the baby bump, enjoying every inch of her changing form.

He sat up on the bed next to her, loosened his tie, and said, "I suppose it's nostalgic for me. When I was a little boy, I would go over to my Grandma and Grandpa's house and they always had it playing. I loved watching it. It was my kind of humor. Now, it reminds me of two people that I love very much. I miss my Grandpa and the time we spent together learning about planes. My Grandma was a fiery redhead just like Lucy."

Melanie sat up and clasped his hand in hers, and said, "Keep it forever. You have my blessing. Lucy is better than bikinis." She blew a kiss at him and he shook his head at her, gently tackling her onto the bed, resuming their kissing.

But there was soon a knock at the door, interrupting.

"James, are you ready to go? We need to leave soon," Bruce said.

"You better get yourself fixed up," Melanie said, running her fingers through his now messy hair. "Your dad is going to wonder what we are doing."

"Mel, you're pregnant with my baby. He *knows* what we are doing," he joked before giving her one more heated kiss.

She giggled as he stood and walked over to the mirror to ready himself once more.

"You look great," she said, admiring him in the mirror. "Too great."

He added more gel to his hair and then walked over to her. "Don't you worry." He leaned down to kiss her softly, but she reached her arms up around his neck and gripped tightly ahold of his shirt collar, feeling like she was holding onto her everything.

After a few moments, he pulled away, saying, "I have to go. Enjoy your evening with my mom and Amber." He poked the tip of her nose with his index finger and walked to the door. As he opened the door to leave, he looked back over his shoulder and said, "Hey Mel? You make me so happy." Then he exited.

She soaked in his words and flopped backwards onto the bed, thinking about how drastically her life had changed these last four months. She'd gone from never having a boyfriend in her whole life to losing her virginity and getting pregnant, and now she was falling madly in love with her best friend's brother! The realization of that hadn't fully occurred to her and she knew she needed to talk to Amber about her relationship with James eventually, though nervous of Amber's true feelings.

"Melanie?" Amber knocked a few minutes later. "Did you still want to go out?"

The disgusted look on Amber's face confused Melanie as she opened the door, until Amber finally said, "Look, Mel, I'm super cool with your relationship with my brother, but could you be a bit more discreet about the fact that you're having sex with him on a very regular basis? Please? Because *that* completely weirds me out." She pointed to Melanie's bare bottom half, and her standing there in only her lacy panties and James's t-shirt.

Melanie's eyes widened as she covered her mouth and she hurried to throw on his sweats, which were on the floor beside the bed. Then she motioned for Amber to come inside.

"*So* sorry! Amber, I'm sorry."

"You're my best friend. He's my only brother and I want his happiness. I want both of you to be happy, really. I'm totally cool with this, but..."

"Really?" Melanie asked as she sat on the bed.

"Yes, really I am. However, I'm going to admit that it's a little weird for me to see you with him. It's YOU, and it's Jamie. I know that's nothing to *you*, but to me it's a lot. Honestly though, if you two are happy, then I'm okay. Especially because..." She lifted Melanie's shirt to take a peek at the growing baby bump. "I'm so excited to meet this little one! I can't wait to meet him! I never thought James would ever have kids. But, he shocked us all." She shrugged. "Get dressed. We'll go get something to eat."

"Okay. Jamie left me his credit card," Melanie said.

"*And* it begins," Amber said, rolling her eyes.

"What?" Melanie asked.

"He is so stingy, but I knew he wouldn't be with you. He never gives anyone a dime. He never buys anything, except that truck of course. But when he fell for you, I knew things would be different. That guy's got money because he never spends any and he's invested well."

"Where does he get his money?" Melanie asked as she stood to get dressed.

"I told you that we inherited a large sum a few years ago," Amber explained.

"Surely it isn't all that much?" Melanie questioned.

"Well, he invested that, but he lives on the interest and he's so smart and he buys and sells all kinds of stocks. When you *do* marry him, you'll never have to work. You'll be a spoiled little NASA wife," Amber said and winked.

Melanie smiled, imagining the thought of that. "Then why does he live here?"

Amber laughed. "I told you. He's cheap." Then she walked out and left Melanie to get changed before they headed to their usual spot at their favorite bar, where Melanie had become very accustomed to eating since being with James, even though it wasn't her favorite by any means.

"What'll you girls have tonight? No James this evening?" the waitress asked as she took their orders.

"No," Melanie responded, wondering why that waitress wanted to know about her man. "I'll have cheese fries and chicken wings."

"Same for me," Amber added as she handed the waitress the menus.

"So, Melanie. I've seen you with James a lot lately. Are you two like... you know, official? Or is he still up for grabs?" the waitress asked.

Melanie snapped her head around and glared at her, responding, "He is NOT up for 'grabs.' Do you not see that I'm very obviously pregnant?" She lifted her shirt and flashed her bump.

The waitress let out a "Huh!" before saying, "Well, that doesn't mean much these days." Then she walked away.

"The many advances and developments that we are making in the technology of the structure and design of this particular type of thrust ..." the Air Force engineer said as he spoke to the crowd, getting reactions from nearly everyone in the audience. Yet, the presenter's engaging speech wasn't enough to keep James interested because all he wanted was to get back to his kissing session with Melanie. It seemed these days she was all that occupied his mind.

"Are you enjoying yourself?" Bruce looked to James as he sipped on a whiskey sour, no cherry.

Only nodding in reply, he discreetly pulled out his phone and sent a text to Melanie:

*Missing you so much right now. Wish we were together. Can't wait until later. You know what I mean. *wink emoji* *

A few minutes later, Melanie responded:

*You naughty boy! You aren't supposed to be texting during the presentation! Are you bored? I miss you too. Behave yourself and I'll reward you greatly. You know what I mean. *kiss emoji* *

He smiled at her response and replied:

I can't wait. I love being rewarded.

His dad looked over and said, "I know you're texting that girl. I was young and in love once too, son."

James slipped his phone away and responded, "Please don't call her 'that girl'. She has a name."

"I apologize, James. I only meant that I feel like you're getting distracted from many of the important things in life. You have goals and a future."

"Dad, she's the mother of my child. She *is* my future."

Bruce turned and faced the presenter, letting the conversation end, not wanting to make a scene.

After the presentation, they headed over to the next room in the conference center where there was a silent auction being held. They browsed a few items and Bruce commented to James on a few of the smaller items.

"This is a nice sail boat. You know, your mom might like a boat. What do you think? You think it's worth $120,000?" Bruce asked.

James shrugged and said, "Don't think you're getting me to pull that thing every time you want it at sea."

Bruce moved on to the next few items until he stopped at another and thought about it for a moment, but James was distracted by his phone once more by a text from Amber:

James! Leave immediately! I'm at the ER with Mel and she's not good! Hurry!

His heart skipped in his chest as he wondered what could be wrong.

"Dad, you stay and enjoy the auction," he said as his dad bid on one of the higher priced items.

"What? Why? What's going on?" Bruce asked.

"Amber just texted to say that Melanie is in the ER again and that I should come right away. I'm getting a cab." He left no time for his dad to protest, but instead he took out his phone and exited the building, impatiently waiting in the front.

"What do you think is wrong?" Janice asked, as the nurses changed Melanie into a clean gown and put some clean pads underneath her to soak up all the blood.

The doctor looked to Janice and motioned to talk to her in the hall.

"Chances are highly likely that her surgery caused some complications and now she's having a late miscarriage."

"But that was weeks ago. She's so far along now. She's got to be 17 weeks pregnant by now."

"Yes. That means her body is going into early labor to dispose of the baby."

Janice began crying, wiping her face with her hands. "She's going to be devastated. We all are."

"Not to judge the situation, but isn't she only like 18 and unwed?" he asked.

Janice looked at him disapprovingly and responded, "That is true, but this baby was very wanted, married or not, young or not. We thought him a blessing. Shame on you."

She walked away and in to see Melanie who was hunched over in pain.

"I'm losing my baby, aren't I?" she asked, teared-up, looking to Janice, who only nodded in reply.

"I know this is early labor," Melanie continued as the cramping came consistently every few minutes. "Ah!" she cried out as she buckled down on the bed and waited for her next dose of pain medication.

James hurried in a short while later to hear shrieks of pain coming from Melanie, and to see the nurse giving her pain meds.

"Her water broke a few minutes ago," Janice explained.

Realizing what that meant, he walked over and grasped her hand. "Mel," he said, unknowing of what else to do or say.

"I guess this means I'm not your girlfriend anymore," she tried joking.

He didn't see the humor in it though, and he replied, "You won't be getting rid of me now."

As he held her hand in his, wishing he could take it away, knowing that she would be delivering a baby who would have no survival chance outside of her, he wanted nothing more than to tell her how he really felt, but he watched as she rocked herself back and forth, trying to ease the relentless cramping, and grimace from the pain, and all he could do was sit there.

"I'm so sorry, Jamie," she cried.

"Me too."

A few hours later, she miscarried a perfectly formed baby boy, and she held him in her hands before the nurses wrapped him up in some cloths.

"What would you have wanted to name him?" she asked with tears dripping from her cheeks while the nurse carried the baby away.

"I don't know. Though I've always dreamed of having a son, I never thought I would because I didn't think about having a wife until I met you."

She sniffled and laid her head on his chest as he wrapped his arms tightly around her, bringing comfort not only to her, but also to himself while they sat on the hospital bed together.

"So, you want a family now?" she asked.

"With you," he answered and kissed the top of her head.

She sighed satisfactorily.

"Jamie. That's what I would name him," she said.

"Jamie?" he asked.

"Yeah. I want him to be just like his dad."

"Yeah. I want a James Tyler Jr.," he agreed.

"Okay," she agreed, "Someday." She leaned up and pulled him in to kiss her, feeling sad but perfectly contented at the same time.

SIX

"Melanie, why don't you want to go to the bar? Are you tired of that food? We can go somewhere else," he asked, wanting her to give him more of an explanation as they dressed for an evening out with friends.

"I don't want to talk about it," she responded.

"Why are you so grumpy? What's going on? Did I do something? Or is this like one of those female things... you know, like PMS?"

She turned back to look at him, eyes penetrating.

"Alright, alright. It's not PMS. Then what is it?"

"I told you. I *don't* want to talk about it," she persisted.

"Fine. Finish getting ready. I'll be in the truck." He walked out of the room and left her to pout on her own.

When she was done fixing her hair, she grabbed her purse off the back of the bedroom door, took a look at herself in her jeans and satin strappy tank that was just starting to fit again— to her own dismay— and she slipped on her shoes. Then she headed outside where she saw him sitting in the truck, leaning back with his hands behind his head.

"Ready?" he asked, extending his hand to help her in as she opened the door.

She situated herself and nodded, giving him the "okay" to drive. But she didn't want to tell him that she was upset about going back to that bar with that waitress. They hadn't been there since she lost the baby weeks ago, and she was feeling very emotional at the idea of exposing herself to that kind of vulnerability.

They walked in and joined his friends, who'd also become hers over the past few months, and they took a seat at the long table. But Melanie's heart nearly stopped, and shock flooded her, when she noticed that the brazen waitress—who was ready to steal her man— was the one who was serving their table tonight

"Hi everyone. What can I get ya'll to drink? Full bar open, or we have coke..." The waitress began listing off their items, but she quickly looked to James and said, "James, should I bring your usual? I know you like that whiskey sour, honey, but no cherry, right?" and gave him a flirtatious wink, blowing him a kiss.

"Yeah, why not start the night off right?" he heartily agreed, but then said, "But I'll have that cherry tonight."

And Willis energetically hollered across the table to him, "Bitch, buy a round of whiskey for all of us! You drive that smokin' truck out there! We know you can afford it!"

James laughed and said, "Hell no! Buy your own damn liquor." Then he looked to the waitress and said, "I'll be paying for only myself. Well, and this cutie right here." And he reached to his side and squeezed Melanie tightly, kissing her cheek, whispering "Get whatever you want, okay?"

"Sure thing, honey," the waitress said before looking to Melanie. "And for *you*?" she asked not as politely.

"Just a sweet tea, please."

"You know, that has a lot of caffeine," she said before turning to take everyone else's orders.

James looked to her, confused, and asked, "Melanie, what did she mean?"

She teared up a bit and answered, "I was here with Amber the night..." she didn't finish but looked away.

He didn't force conversation from her but joined in on the anarchy erupting from everyone else.

James hollered over to his friend.

"Loser?!" he yelled back.

"Did you ever make it over to the Grecian islands this summer with what's her face?" James asked him.

"Yes! You need to go! Take Melanie. It was amazing... Melanie, make him take you."

"Jamie?" she flirted, "I guess we are going on vacation?"

"Ugh..." he groaned, "I guess we are." He winked at Melanie, then looked back across the table. "Thanks. You know I hate commercial airliners."

"Rent a plane!" Willis suggested. "You could fly there in no time."

"You fly?" Melanie looked to Jamie, shocked.

"Thanks a lot," he complained to Willis.

"Yes. I have a pilot's license," he said.

"Why didn't you tell me?" she asked.

"I don't know," he shrugged, avoiding the question.

"Melanie!" Willis hollered to her.

She looked up, forcing a smile, but her attention remained focused on James and his secret keeping.

"I hear you're heading up north with us soon?"

She smiled slightly, looking to James. "Yeah. I'm moving in with you both up there."

Well, hell! Slap my sister and call me pretty! What did this idiot have to do to convince you to move all the way up there? That weather gets pretty terrible compared to this beautiful Atlanta sunshine!"

"Well, my mom lives up there, and..."

"Well, isn't she knocked up with your baby, James?" the waitress asked, returning with the drinks.

Melanie looked away, distraughtly.

71

"Guys, we'll be right back," he said to their friends, and he took Melanie's hand, practically dragging her out to the truck, knowing she was deeply troubled by what the waitress said.

"Did you have a relationship with that woman?" she asked when they got outside.

"Why would you ask me that?" he replied, surprised at her question.

"When I was here with Amber and I was still very obviously pregnant, she *asked* me if you and I were in a relationship or if you were up for grabs!"

He let out a scoff at the waitress's remark and said, "Mel, you can't let everything that others say bother you, babe. Other people are going to get jealous of us all the time. I come to this bar often and she sees me."

"Answer the question!" she yelled.

"We might've... maybe..." he responded, flustered.

"What?!" she widened her eyes and stepped away from him.

"I was completely wasted, Mel. It was nothing. Like, I mean..."

"Like I was..." she nodded. "You used her just like you used me, until you found out I was pregnant."

"No!"

"Goodbye James." She started walking away from him and out of the parking lot to the curb.

"Melanie!" He ran after her.

"Leave me!" She screamed.

"Absolutely not!" He grabbed her arm, pulling her back.

"Let go of me!" She fought back. "I mean it, Jamie!" She started smacking at him to release her arm from his grasp.

"I won't." He insisted before he pulled her face to his and kissed her passionately for several seconds as she continued pushing him back with all her might.

"Go!" she screamed, tears streaming down her face, pushing him away.

"I will not!" he yelled back.

"Just leave me! Go! I'm tired of the lies and the secrets! Just let me go!" she yelled once more, giving him a forceful shove.

He looked to the tears streaming down her face and he realized that he'd done that to her. He wanted to tell her his true feelings, but he didn't know how. Instead, he said, "Fine. Have it your way, stubborn girl. Take some time to cool down. I'll be home later." Then he watched her stomp to the end of the parking lot toward the busy road and disappear into the darkness. Once she was out of sight, he turned and walked back into the bar.

"Where's Melanie?" Willis asked when James returned without her.

"She's not feeling herself. She went home," he answered.

The waitress came to take the rest of the orders and stood directly behind James.

"Hungry tonight?" she whispered, leaning down, noticing Melanie was gone, but he immediately shut her down.

"It's not going to happen, Valerie. You've pissed off my girlfriend and you were rude to her. You're lucky I don't have my sister take you outside and show you how the Hunters get things done. What I did with you in a drunken mistake is nothing compared to what I feel for her. Get over yourself."

She gasped and moved away, but Amber heard him and pulled out her phone to send a text to Melanie:

Jamie just told off that waitress! You should've been here! You would've thought it was hot! He's my brother and I mostly think he's gross, but I admired it!

But a few minutes later Melanie texted back and said:

Tell Jamie that I'm moving my things out. I won't be going to Connecticut with him.

Amber gagged on her fries at the message, which caught James's attention.

"Are you okay?" he asked.

"You need to go home," Amber said.

He took a sip of his whiskey before asking, "What for?"

She didn't say anything but handed her phone across for him to read the message.

Without saying anything else, he handed Amber some cash to pay for his drinks and then he left, hurrying back to his house before she left.

"Melanie!" he rushed upstairs to find her throwing all her clothes in a bag. "What are you doing?!"

She ignored him and continued on.

"Melanie!" he grabbed her arm, turning her to face him. "I asked you a question!"

"You can't just pass out demands. I can leave if I want," she snipped.

"Why are you leaving?" He let go of her arm and sat on the bed next to her bag.

"You never wanted me! There was no afterthought with me. I was only a girl in a bar... just like that waitress. Had I never gotten pregnant, I would've only seen you at Amber's family functions. You lied."

Sighing heavily, he dropped his face into his hands as he did his signature move by resting his elbows on his knees, rocking them back and forth while he contemplated what to say.

"You're right. At first, you were just a girl in a bar. I was home for the weekend and I wanted some sex. I'm surrounded by those stuffy Yale snobs all the time, and when I saw you..."

"And you thought 'Hey! Let me steal this girl's virginity and never call her again'!" She tossed her arms up and continued packing her things.

"No. It wasn't like that. You were a breath of fresh air. I looked at you and honestly thought you were so gorgeous. I had to have you. The way you looked at me, the way you moved and spoke, your smile, all of you. I just knew when Kaylee introduced you that I needed you and I didn't realize you were a virgin, not at first, especially because you were with Kaylee and Amber!"

"But I told you I'd never been on a date," she said.

"Yeah, but by then I was completely taken in by you and wanted you badly. I try to be a nice guy, but I'm still a *guy*. I really think you're the most beautiful girl I've ever seen," he admitted.

She wiped her tears and looked over to where he was sitting. "What's the real reason you never called me, Jamie?"

"I told you about Amber."

"I don't believe you. I want the truth," she demanded.

"I used Amber as an excuse because it seemed legitimate enough. But, I'd never once had a *real relationship* in my whole life and you were giving me feelings that were kind of creepin' me out. I wasn't ready to tell you that I liked you a lot. I also wasn't ready to admit it to myself, I suppose."

He motioned for her to go over to him and he positioned her on his lap. "Mel, please forget about that waitress. It's hard for you to understand because I'm the only guy you've ever been with. But she was only a drunken mistake. I've never thought of her since that night and I have no desire to act on her ever again."

"That's the whole truth?" she asked.

"I swear. You're the girl for me. I've never had the desire for a relationship until now. No one has given me this type of feeling, not until you."

He pulled her closer and whispered, "Please, don't make me beg. But I will if I have to," then he kissed the tip of her nose.

Thinking heavily on his statement she asked, "Hm... should I ask for permission to make the playing deck equal?" She tapped her chin.

"What are you saying?" he tilted his head knowing he wasn't going to like where this was headed.

"Well, how many different women have you been with? Not counting me."

"Eight."

"Eight?! James Tyler Hunter! You cad!"

He laughed softly and said, "Well, I'm a popular guy at my school. There are mostly geeks and nerds up there and it's not too often girls see a fit, muscular, and tall guy, who works out and dresses without suspenders. So, when I walk around on campus, they see brains and beauty." He winked.

"Well! I think that right there is enough to convince me to come with you. Better yet, I'm climbing on your back, riding around with you wherever you go, holding a megaphone, shouting 'Back off chicks! This one's mine!'"

He smiled and said, "I knew I could convince you."

"Now, about making the decks even," she said.

"No way. You are mine."

"Well, I was thinking you could pick the guy. I mean, I don't even know if you're a good lover." She bit her lip innocently, as he pummeled her onto the bed.

After kissing a few minutes, he sat up and asked, "Does this mean you're staying?"

She nodded, but then she asked, "Where were you with that waitress? Did you bring her here?"

Groaning, he replied, "My truck."

Sitting up quickly and cupping his face in her hands, she said, "I've never been in your truck with you."

"Is *that* how we can drop this subject? Because I'll take your ass out there in my dad's driveway right now."

"No," she said, "But I want two truck romps. I'm special."

He smirked and said, "You've got yourself a *very* irresistible deal."

"Okay. I'll take that deal. But, what was it about those other girls that interested you?" She got up and walked over to his dresser where he had a picture of her in a frame.

"They were available, moderately attractive, had all their teeth, could speak in semi-intelligent sentences, and I was either really desperate or..."

"Or?" she turned to face him.

"Drunk, Mel. It doesn't take much to grab a guy's attention when he's drunk."

"Gee, thanks."

"I wasn't drunk when I met you. I had one whiskey sour. That's all. I legitimately liked the way you looked. You honestly turned my head."

"How did you hook up with that waitress?" she turned back to look at the picture on his dresser, which was his favorite because he took it of her while she was sitting on that wooden bridge.

"I was there with Willis and Kaylee. That was about two years ago when they were dating."

"How old was Kaylee?"

"She was 19 at the time, but they broke up shortly after. I was home on winter break and Willis and I were there for a good long while before Kaylee showed up and I'd had too many whiskeys. He left me there alone and I was bored. That's all, Melanie. It didn't mean anything."

"Then why was she so rude to me?" Melanie asked as she walked back over and sat on his lap, James wrapping his arms around her, pulling her in close.

"The next time I went in, which was a few days later I think, she acted like I owed her something. But I completely blew her off, acting exactly like what it was—a one-night stand. But she wanted it to go further. I wasn't interested in her at all."

"Oh."

"Hey, could you just understand that though this didn't begin the way you think it should've, my feelings for you now are really strong. Could you?"

"I'll try."

He pulled her back onto him and began caressing her back as he moved to lift her shirt over her head, disappearing under the covers together.

"Melanie," he said while she ran her fingers through his hair after their passion filled lovemaking. "Maybe I've been with eight other women, but none have given me satisfaction like that. I can't get enough of you." He kissed down the front of her, taking in all her beauty. "You're really so much different to me."

She moved her hands to hold his face as he continued kissing, but then she took his chin in her palm, pulling it up, forcing him look her in the eyes and she replied, "I want you to know something, something very important."

"Alright."

But as she stared into his beautiful eyes, her nerves were on edge and she paused for a moment to think on whether or not she should tell him her true feelings, because he hadn't declared love for her.

"What is it?" he asked, moving up and leaning in for a soft kiss.

"Nothing. Never mind," she said, ultimately deciding that she shouldn't.

SEVEN

"Do you have all your things ready? The truck is out front. All my stuff is loaded, ready to go," James said as he peeked his head inside the bedroom door to see Melanie sitting on the bed holding her jacket.

"I'm ready," she said.

"Melanie?" He opened the door and walked inside. "Is everything okay?"

She breathed deeply and nodded.

"I don't believe you. What's wrong?"

"I don't want to tell you because you're just going to get angry," she responded.

"I'm not going to get angry. Tell me what's wrong." He walked over and sat next to her.

"Well, I was moving because of the baby, but we aren't having a baby now and..."

"Don't you want to come?" he asked, standing, confused at her sudden change in emotions.

"Well, I've grown quite used to Atlanta, and Amber is here, and..."

"I see." He turned and walked out.

"Jamie!" she called after him. "Jamie!" She huffed at his stubbornness and refusal to listen to her, but still decided to walk out after him, only to be met by him in the doorway.

"Melanie, I won't force you to come, though I want you to, but I want you to know that for *me*, you coming up there wasn't completely about the baby. However, now that I find out *your* intentions, mine are changing."

"Wha..." she stuttered.

"Stay with Amber." He walked out, leaving her in a confused daze. But after she gathered her thoughts, she raced down the stairs and watched out the door just in time to see him drive away.

Weeks went by without a word from him, and she was beginning to feel hopeless at the situation, regretting her decision.

"Why don't you call him?" Amber asked when she walked into the bedroom one evening to comfort the weeping ball of sadness which had become Melanie.

"He left me here. There's a reason he hasn't called. I'm not going to be desperate. He's moved on," she whimpered.

"Well, Mel, you can't stay this way forever. What do we need to do for you?"

"Just leave me here." She pushed Amber away and covered herself in the blankets.

"Oh Melanie..." Amber rolled her eyes and walked out.

Melanie decided to comfort herself by snooping through social media, hoping to find out if James had truly moved on. Though she wasn't *actually* ready to accept the idea that he might have a new girlfriend, something inside her still wanted to find out. So, the search began.

She immediately searched through her followers on Instagram until she found his— @Jmsplswskyrkts90— and she clicked on it, hoping he'd made new posts, so she could see what he'd been up to.

But after looking through his endless photos of planes, some of him studying, working out, and a couple of him with Willis drinking, or of his truck, but also few of them together, she realized that his last post was with her, as she was tagged in it—@Melanyswts95. Liking that pic of them together and not having noticed it before, she tapped the heart, hoping he wouldn't notice. However, much to her immediate panic, he must've been right near his phone because he instantly sent her a direct message.

Hey. I saw you liked our picture. It's a good one. Are you trying to tell me something?

Still unsure why he hadn't called and not wanting to seem like the desperate one, she replied:

It was a good night.

She didn't say more, but continued scrolling through, admiring him as she laid in her misery.

TWO WEEKS LATER

"Amber?" she said one morning as she walked down to have breakfast.

"Hey there. Are you going to mope around mourning the loss of James forever? Or are you going to do something with your newly graduated self? My mom said she can get you a job at her firm. I know! Let's move out of this house and get you out of his room. We should get an apartment!"

Melanie nodded enthusiastically at the suggestion of being out on her own, and they began plans for that immediately. When Janice came home that afternoon, she spoke to her about a job.

"Amber says you have some openings at your firm?" Melanie asked.

"I can get you a job as an assistant," Janice offered as she walked inside and sat her things on the kitchen counter.

"What would I be doing?"

"Sorting files, basic paperwork, answering phones and keeping schedules... simple things. You would make enough for you and Amber to move out, if that's what you were thinking."

Melanie nodded and looked to Amber, and they squealed excitedly together.

"This apartment has two bedrooms. The kitchen is small, but the bathroom is a decent size for two girls who will be sharing it together," the realtor said, as Melanie and Amber walked the apartment together with Bruce and Greg, who both wanted to be sure the girls weren't getting ripped off.

"How much?" Bruce asked.

"$2750 a month, plus all utilities," he replied.

"Tell the landlord that for $2350 he can consider himself lucky because this place is hardly 1500 square feet and with the few modern amenities that it has..." Bruce continued criticizing, as Amber pulled Melanie's arm and walked away into the front entry.

"Mel, my brother texted yesterday to tell me he's coming into town for Thanksgiving."

"So? Who's he to me now?" Melanie rolled her eyes.

"I just wanted you to know. Listen, I was hoping you would have Thanksgiving with us since your dad always leaves to his mom's on holidays and your mom is spending it with her husband and I know you don't want to be *there*. But I don't want things to be awkward for you."

"It won't be awkward. I love your family as if they were my own."

"Okay. If you're sure." Amber nodded.

"I'm sure. I'll be there."

At the end of the month, the girls moved into the apartment and touched up everything to their liking, and by Thanksgiving, Melanie was feeling much better about dealing with James at the Hunter family Thanksgiving festivities.

"Mel, do you want the sofa here or there?" Amber asked as she stood on one side of the living room, contemplating where to position the furniture.

"Um... I think I like it there," she pointed to the wall next to the window.

"What about the coffee table my mom bought? Here or... here?" Amber's phone beeped. "Hold on. You move it, while I answer this text."

Jamie: *How is Melanie? Did you invite her to Thanksgiving dinner? I have a surprise for her. Do you think there's any chance at all?*

Amber watched Melanie nonchalantly move around the furniture as though she had not a care in the world, and Amber was thinking that she was completely over James by now. But she didn't have the heart to tell him that. So, she only replied:

I'm not a mind-reader! I guess you'll have to come and find out. BTW you should've called her!

They finished moving around the furniture and Amber finally got the courage to ask, "Hey. Are things going to be okay, you know, with James?"

"Oh yeah. I've finally come to terms with what I was to him. I'm over it."

Amber sighed and realized that Melanie had no idea. None at all.

"Janice?" Melanie asked a few days later while she was finishing up filing at the office.

"Yes? How can I help?" Janice asked. "Are you not finished with the documents of the Turner case? It can wait until after the holiday." She waved for Melanie to cease filing and leave.

"Actually, I was just wondering if there was anything I can bring to dinner tomorrow. I know there will be extra mouths for you to feed and I wanted to help."

"Aren't you sweet? You don't need to bring anything but yourself. However, you know my kitchen well and if you'd like to come early and help me set things up, Amber and I would love the extra company. Kaylee won't be home from school for break, so it's just me and Amber. Well, and James of course, but you know all he does is eat," she said, but then looked to Melanie cautiously.

"It's okay, Janice. I'm okay about him. Of course I'll come help," she said.

Janice nodded, tapping the desk, "I'm heading out for the evening sweetie. Now, you don't stay too late. Alright?"

"Okay."

Melanie finished up her work and gathered her things to leave but was approached by someone on her way to the elevator.

"Melanie, I've been meaning to talk to you," one of the attorneys said as he walked up behind her.

"I finished all the files for the Turner case, Mr. Burkhart," she responded.

"Please, it's Nick. Mr. Burkhart makes me feel like my dad. I'm not even 30."

"What did you need?" she asked, stepping onto the elevator.

"Well, I was wondering if you'd like to have dinner?" he asked as he stepped onto the elevator with her.

Meanwhile, James arrived into town that evening with Willis at about 5:00pm.

"Mom! What's there to eat around here?" he shouted as they walked inside.

"Hi, baby! Hi, Willis! I've got nothing! Tomorrow's Thanksgiving and all my ovens are occupied! Go to that bar you like so much!" she hollered back.

"Where's Amber?" he asked, walking into the kitchen where Janice was speckled with the obvious mess of Thanksgiving preparations.

"She's at her apartment. Didn't she tell you she moved out and got an apartment with Melanie?"

"No." He crossed his arms, feeling upset at the absence of Melanie.

"Melanie is working at my firm and Amber works at some fashion boutique in town selling designer bridal gowns."

"Later, Mom." He walked away, not wanting to hear any more.

He dialed Amber when he got into the truck, receiving her voicemail.

"Hi ya'll. It's Amber. Leave me a message and I'll get back to ya later."

"I'm going to the bar. You have explaining to do."

"What's wrong, man?" Willis asked while they drove into the bar's lot, noticing James's scowl and his bitter attitude on the phone with Amber.

"I should've called her," James said to Willis.

"I told you that much. You've been miserable."

"Yeah well, she got an apartment with Amber. She's moving on."

They walked in and James approached the bar, his eyes and mind fixed on the whiskey and exactly how much he was going to consume to get his mind off Melanie.

"James!" the bartender said. "How's life up in the north?"

"Hit me hard tonight, Bobby."

"That bad?" he replied.

"Straight up. No sour... not tonight."

The bartender nodded and turned to get his whiskey, while James turned to look around the bar, when he noticed Melanie in the far corner with a man.

"Willis," James said.

"Yeah?" he turned around on his stool, holding his beer. But immediately he saw what James was seeing and felt frustrated for his friend. "Want to find another bar? Want me to deck the little fancy man in the face? What you want me to do? Tell me lover," Willis joked, but he soon realized James was really distraught and was fighting an urge to go over there and punch the man wearing the fancy suit. So he added, "In all seriousness, my friend, I can see you're upset. What do you want me to do? I'll lay him out on the floor, if that's what it'll take."

James sighed slightly at his friend's remark before he said, "Nothing. Do nothing. She's obviously not my girlfriend anymore. She has the right to see or *do* whoever she wants. I have no claim on her, not anymore."

"Well, okay then, bitch," Willis said. "Let's just get wasted. Forget her!"

James turned around, downing his first whiskey, sighing at the bitter satisfaction it brought, admiring how gorgeous he thought Melanie looked in her emerald-colored dress, which she'd obviously worn to work. But after a few shots, he looked back at Melanie again as she engaged in conversation with the other man, who he'd figured was an attorney from his mother's firm, and his stomach lurched over the thought that she was sitting there happily in another man's company. James faced toward the bar and reached his arm out to hold up his glass for another. "Hit me with another, Bobby!"

Many shots of whiskey later, Bobby called it quits on him, telling Willis they needed to call a driver to take him home.

But James protested. "Nah, I'm okay. I still have some life left in me. Look!" And he stood and stumbled over to the jukebox, holding his glass. "This is perfect, Will!"

And the song began to play while James loudly sang along...

"Blame it all on my roots, I showed up in boots, and ruined your black tie affair.

The last one to know, the last one to show, I was the last one, you thought you'd see there.

And I saw the surprise, and the fear in his eyes,

When I took his glass of champagne, and I toasted you, said, honey, we may be through, but you'll never hear me complain..."

And he held his glass up toward her, as if he were gesturing to toast her, then downed his shot and slammed the glass onto the bar floor, shattering it into a thousand pieces, capturing Melanie's attention, along with everyone else's.

"I've got friends in low places, where the whiskey drowns and the beer chases my blues away. I'll be okay..." he continued to sing along to Garth Brooks's song.

Willis walked over to where James stood resting his arm at the jukebox. "She's looking over this way. She sees you, man." And he helped James back to the barstool before he fell over, and Melanie watched him stumble back to the bar.

"Look how drunk that redneck hick is," Nick shook his head shamefully at James. "Honestly, Melanie, I don't see the appeal of this bar. What is it you like about this place? It's nothing but a dirty honky tonk to me," Nick commented to her as they watched Willis pick James back up after falling onto the floor.

Thinking how rude Nick's comment was, she didn't respond but stood to leave, not wanting to watch this display from James anymore.

"Willis, give me my keys, damnit!" James yelled, catching Melanie's attention once again.

"James, it's my call," the bartender said, and Melanie listened in as she was walking to the door. She saw Willis and James arguing, and she stopped at the door to hear more.

"C'mon buddy. I'll call your mom," Willis said, reaching for the keys once more.

"Lay off, Willis!" James yelled far too loudly. But Willis insisted.

"I'm not giving in," he said and pulled out his cell. "I'm dialing Janice."

"No! Back off!" James yelled, shoving him.

Seeing that, Melanie looked to Nick and said, "I had a nice time and I appreciated your invitation for dinner, but..." She glanced over to see James reaching for his shot glass once more.

"But?"

"I have something I need to deal with. I have to go. It's not you," she convinced as she continued watching James out of the corner of her eye.

"Have a good night, Melanie. Perhaps another time." Nick kissed her cheek and walked out.

She stomped over to James and Willis, exclaiming, "James Tyler! What is going on over here?! You are causing a scene for the whole bar to see! Willis, give me those keys." She grabbed the shot glass from James's hand and held out her hand for the truck keys, saying, "I'll take him home."

Willis smiled, and complied, handing her the keys. "Yes, Ma'am."

She looked angrily to James, who sat back down and laid his head down on the bar.

"James Tyler!" She gripped his jaw between her thumb and index finger, forcing him to look at her.

"Melanie..." He grinned. "Hey, good lookin'." He winked sloppily and tried to kiss her.

"Don't you start with me," she scolded. "I can't believe you were going to try and drive home tonight! Why would you do that?! There are people who love and care about you!"

"But not you." His face saddened as he stood and fell forward onto her, forcing her to steady him in her arms.

"What?" She asked, moving his face to look her in the eyes.

"You... you don't care," he muttered before he passed out on the floor.

"I've got him," Willis said, walking over, throwing him onto his shoulder and carrying him out to the truck.

"What was this all about tonight, Willis?" she asked as she drove him to *her* apartment instead of Janice's house, so not to worry Janice at the arrival of a passed-out James.

"I think you two need to discuss that."

"Tell me," she demanded.

"He was a mess at school. He couldn't concentrate and started forgetting assignments and instead of getting all A's as he used to, he was getting B's, and then C's," Willis said.

"Why?" she asked.

"You."

She whipped her head around in his direction. "What *about* me?"

"I think he loves you," Willis said with a shrug.

"But he didn't call. Why didn't he call?"

"He must've felt you made your decision, is all I can figure. I've known this guy a long time and he can be pretty stubborn. But, Melanie?"

"Yeah?" she asked.

91

"He also has a heart of gold," Willis added before he hopped out of the truck, opening the back door to carry James inside as she parked in front of the apartment building.

"Where do you want him?" Willis asked once inside, and she pointed to her room.

"Do you need a ride?" she asked.

"Nah, I'm good. Goodnight, Melanie. I hope you two get this figured out."

"Thanks Willis. You're such a good friend to him," she said, kissing his cheek as he turned to leave.

She checked around for Amber but noticed she wasn't home, thankfully. Then she walked to her bedroom and saw James was still passed out but also filthy from lying on the bar floor, so she decided to make him more comfortable, and she struggled to undress his 6 foot 2 inch, 190 pound, muscular frame.

"There ya go, big guy," she said as she stripped off his boots, t-shirt, and jeans, and left him to lay on her bed in only his boxers. "Take a rest." She sighed and kissed his forehead, running her fingers through his hair, pausing to notice how handsome she still thought he was. But she quickly changed her thoughts, remembering how she'd cried herself to sleep these past many weeks.

She stood and took some of her clothes out of the dresser, but he leaned up on his elbows.

"Melanie," he said groggily.

"Yeah?" she answered, turning to face him.

"Do you miss me?" he asked.

"Why don't you just get some sleep?" she suggested.

"Come and lay with me." He patted the bed next to him.

She sighed, feeling like he was sucking her back in, so she shook her head and reached for the door knob.

"Mel... please." He begged, but she walked out and to the bathroom to change.

After putting on the Bulldogs t-shirt and a pair of his boxers that he'd mistakenly left behind, she brushed her teeth and contemplated sleeping on the couch. But she peeked in to see that he was sawing logs, so she quietly walked to the opposite side of her bed and climbed in next to him, intertwining his fingers in hers under the blankets.

"I missed you every day," she said, resting her head on his shoulder. "It hurts without you. I love you." She fell asleep right there.

"Melanie? Did you go out with a guy last night? It reeked of man's cologne and whiskey when I came in last night," Amber asked the next morning while they were getting ready to head to Janice's for Thanksgiving dinner.

"It's not what you think. Don't jump to any conclusions," Melanie said, taking Amber's arm and dragging her down the hall. "Now, promise you're not going to freak out."

"Melanie..." Amber began and opened the door to see James sleeping on Melanie's bed, and she immediately spun around, angry.

"What is this?!" She tossed her hands up. "I thought you said you were over him?! That isn't what it looks like to me! It *looks* you were under him! Get out here, missy." She pulled Melanie out to the living room and sat her down on their navy-blue sofa. "Explain yourself."

"It isn't what you think, really. I was on a date with one of the lawyers at your mom's firm and..."

"And I got drunker than Cooter *fuckin'* Brown, Amber," James said, stressing his already strong southern accent— which Melanie happened to find irresistible— as he moseyed into the kitchen, that was an open floorplan to the living room with an attached breakfast bar, and he opened the fridge to look for something to eat.

"What *are* you talking about?" Amber asked. "And how many times do I *have* to tell you *not* to come in here looking like that?!" She pointed to him in only his boxers.

"What I'm *sayin'* is that I went to the bar to get a little drunk with my *friend*. But then I got there and..." He turned and looked to Melanie, who was sitting with her arms crossed over her chest, crying. "Well, isn't this perfect?" He rolled his eyes and looked away. "And where in the lovin' hell is all the food around here?!" he yelled. "Yogurt?! No one wants to eat this shit! Where's the *man* food?!"

"James," Melanie said, getting up to walk over to him, "The cereal you like is right up there, but why don't you get a shower first? Come on." She took his hand, leading him into her bedroom. "You are *so* hung over. I'll get you some Advil and water while you shower."

In her bedroom, she got out a pair of his sweats and grabbed an old t-shirt of his from her drawer. "Here, put this on when you get out."

"You've still got those? And you're still wearing my Bulldogs shirt?"

"I like it," she said.

"I heard what you said last night," he said, opening the door, looking back over his shoulder.

"About?" she asked.

He slammed the door shut and walked back over to her, tossing the clothes onto the bed. "Why were you out with that fancy man, Mel?" He grasped her hand in his and held her face, gently playing with her earlobe.

"I don't know." She shook her head. "You never called. My heart was hurting and I... I guess I'm tired of feeling like a one night stand."

"Melanie, you're not a one night stand to me."

"But..."

"I love you! I always have. I'm just a shit head. You know I am. Please, come to Connecticut. It's not the same anymore. You're home to me now."

"Did you mean that?" she asked, teary-eyed.

"What's that?"

"You love me?"

"I do. I've loved you so long, but I didn't know it for sure until I didn't have you anymore. I've been such a mess without you. I need you in my life, baby. It's got to be you and me, always. I love you. Come with me. Stay with me."

"What's it going to be like there? And what about Amber? We have this apartment now and..."

He held her finger to her lips to shush her. "I'll figure something out; just say you'll come. I don't want to see you with any other fancy suit lawyers. I want you with me." He pointed from her to himself. Then, holding up his middle and pointer finger, one crossed over the other, linked onto the other, he said, "We belong together."

"Tell me why you didn't call," she said.

"I thought you made up your mind. I felt like you needed your space. I'm not good at this boyfriend thing. I'm learning," he replied.

"That's what Willis said," she responded.

"What did he say?" he asked.

"That you thought I'd made up my mind," she said.

"That S.O.B. is making me look bad," he said, shaking his head.

"He's a good friend to you," she said, reaching up to kiss the tip of his nose.

"Ha. Yeah, one who rats me out to my girlfriend and sleeps with my sister."

"What?"

"Yeah. I think he's involved with Kaylee again."

"No, I mean, do you want me to be official again?"

"Of course I do. I never considered us broken up. Seeing you with that guy devastated me."

"Oh. I'm sorry, Jamie." She wrapped her arms around him tightly. "So, you didn't add to your playing deck while you've been away?"

"NO! I was miserable. I missed you a lot. I won't ever recover from these big chocolate brown eyes." He gently brushed his thumb over her eyelid, kissing it. "I'm wrapped around your finger." He took her finger in his.

"James, I didn't go because I was afraid. I couldn't let my heart go into the unknown. I wasn't sure what it was going to be like there and I was unsure of your feelings for me."

"Now you have no excuse." He kissed her forehead.

"We better get ready. Your mom is expecting me soon." She stood and walked to the door.

"Hey," he said as she pulled it open to leave.

"Yeah?"

"Why do you have the cereal I like? You don't eat it," he pointed out.

"Wishful thinking," she replied with a playful smile.

"Leave the bathroom unlocked," he said as he quickly grabbed up his things to follow behind her.

EIGHT

"James!" Amber hollered as she peeled potatoes in the kitchen.

"What could possibly be so important than you find it necessary to interrupt the game? This is man's time! Do your woman's thing and we'll do our man's thing!" he yelled back as Willis shouted at the TV from a bad play happening. "But Mel, baby, be a doll and bring us some food?" he turned and blew her a kiss. Melanie rolled her eyes, sticking out her tongue, while Amber continued with her questioning.

"Why haven't you told Melanie about her surprise?" she asked.

James turned around, giving her a "shut the hell up" look and he said, "Well, because that defeats the purpose of a *surprise*, but some meddling sister of mine can't keep her big mouth shut."

"What is it?" Melanie asked looking back and forth between the two of them. "Now you *have* to tell me! Jamie!"

"You can wait and see," he turned around and faced the TV once more, taking a drink of his beer.

"Amber! Tell me what it is!" Melanie shouted.

"Nope," Amber said, looking to James.

"You're gonna find out in a few days. Just be patient," James yelled out to her.

"But I don't want to wait a few days," she said, walking into the living room, grabbing the beer out of his hand, sitting on his lap. "I want to know *now.*" She kissed him, trying to change his mind.

"Aw hell," Willis complained. "Why ya'll gotta be doin' that shit? The kids are watchin'."

James picked up the remote and tossed it at his head, while Melanie kissed on James's cheek and earlobe, moving her hands under his t-shirt.

"Please?" she whispered into his ear, nibbling on it some more, stirring some soft moans of frustration from him.

He pulled her face down and kissed her lips, then he whispered, "Fine. I'll do it if you let me take you upstairs right now."

A small gasp escaped from her mouth and she scolded, "James Tyler! That's naughty!"

"You are driving me crazy, woman," he groaned and kissed her earlobe once more.

"Knock off that nasty talk!" Willis shouted to them. "There will be none of that until the kids go to bed!"

James laughed, tossing his beer bottle at him, but he ducked and it flew over his head and crashed into the wall instead, causing Janice to emerge from where she'd been in the den.

"Shit!" James whispered, laughing.

"Now you're in trouble," Willis laughed.

"What was that noise?" Janice asked. "What are you boys doing out here? Melanie? Are they goofin' around? I'm counting on you to keep them in line now. Ya hear?" She smiled and walked into the kitchen.

"It's okay," Melanie said, standing. "I'll get it cleaned up." She reprimanded James with her eyes.

"How's everything in the kitchen? Amber?" Janice walked out while Melanie grabbed the broom to sweep up the broken glass.

"James!" Bruce walked in with his brother, Norman— who looked exactly like him, with tall, lanky features and dark hair—

and his wife, Betty, a chubbier, rounded, bob-haired, blonde woman.

"Hi, Dad. Hi, Uncle Norm. Hi, Aunt Betty."

Bruce rushed over to James, looking around before he spoke, while Norman sat on the other couch with Willis immersing himself in the game, and Betty joined the ladies in the kitchen.

"Where's Melanie?" he whispered.

"In the kitchen. Why?" James answered.

"Do you remember a little while back when we were at that benefit and I put in a bid on an item?"

"Yeah. Dad... I hope it wasn't that damn sail boat," he complained, thinking that he was going to have to pull it for his dad, since Bruce drove a measly little five passenger car.

"No! I bought an airplane."

James quickly turned his head around to look his dad in the eyes. "Are you shittin' me?"

"You're damn right I did! I bought it for you James! Now you can get your flight hours in for NASA!" Bruce proclaimed.

"Dad! You crazy ass son of a bitch!" James jumped up enthusiastically, grinning. "I can't believe you!" He hugged Bruce and shouted out happily again, as he caught the attention of the ladies in the kitchen and also Melanie who was walking back in to clean up the mess.

"What's all the excitement in here?" she asked but was interrupted by Betty who was following closely behind to bring in refreshments for the men watching football.

"James! Why didn't you tell your Aunt that your girlfriend was so darlin'? Oh, my goodness! I could just eat her up!"

"Aunt Betty," James shook his head disapprovingly.

"Aw now, don't be embarrassed. I know that Melanie here is a northern girl and she's not used to our sweet hospitality, but if she's going to be in this family then she'd better damn well get used to it." Betty went over to Melanie, holding her face, planting a kiss on her cheek.

"Ugh. Aunt Betty," James shook his head shamefully, hanging his face in his palm.

"It's okay, Jamie." Melanie looked to Betty and said, "I appreciate that you are all so kind to me." Then she walked over to James and said, "Now, what was all that commotion? You were pretty excited about something."

"Mel! You'll never believe it!" he exclaimed.

"Okay but try me," she said.

"I always wanted to reach for the stars and I've been trying since the day I hit high school and decided to apply to Yale's science department."

"Okay."

"I know I'm headed for the moon now, baby!" he yelled excitedly.

"Would you just come out with it?"

"Dad bought me my own plane! No more rentals or practice courses!" he exclaimed, picking her up and twirling her around.

"Oh my god! Jamie! AH!!!" she squealed excitedly, wrapping her arms tightly around him.

"When do we get to see it?" she asked, looking to Bruce.

"Better yet, Dad, when do I get to fly it?" James asked, putting Melanie down.

"I'm making preparations to have it to Atlanta within the week," Bruce responded as sat on the couch and grabbed some pickles off the tray on the coffee table.

Melanie squealed happily and jumped back up into James's arms, wrapping her legs around his waist, throwing her arms around his neck, hugging him.

"How about taking me upstairs now?" she whispered in his ear.

Grinning happily, he whispered back, "Gladly."

He started to carry her across the living room to head upstairs, receiving some shouts from Willis and Bruce as he blocked the game, but continuing on, nonetheless.

However, he caught the attention from his mother when he got to stairway and she noticed him leaving.

"And just where do ya'll think you are headed?"

"Um..." was all he could manage to utter.

"Get your buns back in here! We are not cooking up all this food for you to just go to foolin' around. We're fixin' to eat and I know ya'll are going to be rootin' around for something later."

"Yes ma'am," he said to her, but discreetly winked to Melanie, carrying her into the dining room, setting her down on a chair.

"Now, how about helping out while I put out a spread."

"Mom, did you make that salad?" James asked.

"Oh Jamie, that stuff is terrible," Amber criticized.

"What is?" Melanie asked.

"Of course I made it, baby. I know you love it," Janice said.

James smiled and said, "She always makes me this salad."

"I can't wait to taste it," Melanie said, clutching his arm, looking admiringly up at his gorgeous eyes.

"Dad! Where's your whiskey?" he hollered.

"I'm out!" Bruce hollered back.

"What?! What's a holiday without the proper liquor?" James complained.

Melanie sighed at his love for whiskey, but admired it all the same.

"I have Pepsi and there are lemons right there," Janice said. "And here's your pea salad."

"Yum. Thanks." He grinned and looked to Melanie. "Try some."

She took a bite, thinking how terrible it was, but looked to James as he was shoveling it in and she smiled, taking another bite too. Then she watched him grab up the Pepsi and a few lemons, squirting the juice of the lemons right into his Pepsi, and she thought how terrible that must be, so she took a sip and cringed at the taste, then washed the flavor down with her delicious sweet tea.

"What'd you think?" he asked, anticipating her response.

"Wonderful. Just like you," she kissed his cheek and went right back to learning all about him.

"Alright, ya'll!" Janice yelled as she placed the turkey in the center of the table. "Food's ready!"

"But the game isn't over!" Bruce and Norm yelled back.

"Get in here!" she ordered.

Willis was quickly at the table to get his share, and the others were soon to follow.

"So, Melanie," Betty began, "Janice tells us that you graduated Salutatorian. That's quite an accomplishment. Did James tell you he was Valedictorian?"

"He did not, but I saw his picture in the high school," Melanie replied, glancing over to him as he shoveled his face full of turkey, mashed potatoes, and the rest of Thanksgiving fixings.

"With grades like yours, why is it that you aren't attending some big-time school somewhere like James?" Norman asked.

She stared at Norman for a moment and thought about how much he looked like his brother before she answered, "Well, most colleges require *money* to attend, and with my parents being divorced, that situation is more complicated for me because I didn't want massive amounts of student debt. Also, I haven't really made up my mind on the career choice I want in life, and I figured, why waste my money on an expensive education just because everyone says I should?"

James smiled at her response, thinking it very wise, and he added, "Plus, she has me. Who needs a job when you have a moderately attractive, *mostly* socially acceptable, all-the-time available, sugar daddy?"

Willis laughed so hard that beer and mashed potatoes squirted out of his nose. Amber rolled her eyes letting out a disgusted grunt, and Janice and Bruce looked to each other sighing.

The rest of dinner was generally, peaceful, until Melanie asked, "Is it nap time?" as she finished off her piece of pecan pie.

And James responded, "Sure. Why don't I take you upstairs *now*?"

"Okay, if you tell me my surprise."

He leaned in and whispered, "No."

"It's not like she can't find it anyway, Jamie. She wears your clothes," Amber shrugged.

At Ambers words, Melanie jumped up and raced to the stairs, with James following quickly behind.

"Thanks a lot!" James hollered back to Amber.

"Melanie! NO!" he yelled, running up the stairs behind Melanie, while she ran into the bedroom and started fishing through the drawers of his dresser, tearing out the shirts, pants, and boxers... rooting around in all the corners, trying to search for whatever it was that he was hiding from her.

He hurried inside and grabbed ahold of her just as she found a small square jewelry box.

"Jamie?" she said, pulling the box from underneath his jeans and out of his drawer.

"I didn't know if I stood a chance of getting you back, but I wanted to try." He walked over and took the box from her hand. "I told you I'm new at this boyfriend thing, and I've never had feelings like this ever before in my life, nor have I had the desire to even want them. Melanie, before I met you, I was only focused on one thing—school and my career—women were just a luxury to me that I used in passing. But then I met you and everything changed."

He opened the box and showed her a dazzling heart shaped gold pendant with diamonds all along one side and dangling behind was another heart—a solid gold one—engraved with "J&M" and "5/11/13," which was the day they met.

"I just love you, and I want you to know it." He put the necklace on her, kissing her earlobe as he clasped the gold chain. "Please don't doubt my feelings for you anymore. I'm going to mess up a lot. I know I will, but my intentions will never be less than honorable. Alright?"

She turned to face him, cupping his face in her hands, "Alright. Let's just always be ridiculously happy. I don't like it when you're not here. It makes me sad," she said.

"I'm going to do my best. Come on. Mom's going to want to see the surprise."

"You mean, you picked it out?" she asked.

"Yes. Surprised? It was supposed to be for your birthday. Do you like it?"

"Very much."

NINE

"I'd rather stay with you," he said, turning to kiss her, before grabbing his bag full of books and his computer.

"I think I'll check out the library today instead of taking the truck to go shopping. Give me your pass and then text me when you need to get in," she held out her hand and he gave her his restricted access student pass.

"Hey Mel?"

"Yeah?"

"Which library?"

She looked at him, overwhelmed at the size of the school, and he said, "Try the medical library. You'd like that one," and he turned and kissed her again before he left his apartment for class.

Melanie immediately sent a text to Amber:

It sucks here. I miss Atlanta. Rescue me?

Then she got dressed, just throwing on her regulars— a t-shirt and jeans— and she grabbed a coat and some mittens to brave the northern January, then she headed out the door to find the library.

"Where are the medical journals?" she asked one of the library aids when she arrived.

"Third floor."

"Thank you."

Amber texted back just then:

Sorry you're not liking it there. How are things with Jamie? You can always come home. I don't like living with my cousin. She's a prude and doesn't let me bring guys around! She's like into Jesus and things and gets up early to pray for me saying,

"And God bless Amber and her sinful ways..." I can't take this shit, Mel!

Melanie laughed at Amber's comment and replied:

Lol. That is rough! But it could be worse. It could be Kaylee and her incessant need to clean everything! I miss you. Come for a visit soon. Things are okay, I guess. I have news.

But she decided to leave Amber hanging with suspense and waited to tell her more later, and she started fishing through some of the journals and took a seat, waiting for James to finish his class rotation.

"Why do you look familiar?" a girl said, taking a seat across from Melanie, setting her bag down, opening up a book labeled, *The Human Brain, Figuring People Out.*

"I'm not sure. I'm not a student here..." Melanie began, but the girl interrupted.

"Oh! Now I know. I've seen your picture. Do you know James Hunter?"

Melanie's heart froze in her chest and nearly stopped beating as she stared at the red-haired, green-eyed beauty of a girl.

"No," she replied and grabbed her things, then sped out of that library faster than she'd ever thought possible, fearing that everything had all been a lie and that she'd been tricked. When she got outside, she stood with her back to the stone wall, gripping the necklace around her neck for a few minutes to catch her breath and let her heartbeat slow. Then, when she was certain she wasn't going to pass out on the concrete, she slowly walked to the bench.

I Love Lucy my ass, Jamie... I'm pretty sure I just met your fiery red head. All of this has been a lie! Did you think I wouldn't find out?! Did you think I wouldn't meet her?! First the redheaded waitress, now this girl...

Melanie berated him in her mind as she walked off campus and down a few blocks away to a local coffee shop, where she drank her sorrows away.

"A latte. Decaf please."

And she sat, wallowing in her misery, thinking that James had deceived her. When the first latte was gone, she ordered another.

A few hours later, James texted her:

Hey babe, I'm done. Where are you? Hungry? What are you in the mood for today?

Not wanting to speak to him, she turned off her phone, laid down her head and cried, still clutching ahold of her necklace.

A little while later, after she'd fallen asleep for a decent amount of time, one of the workers of the cafe approached her, "Are you okay? Did you need anything else? We're about to close."

"Oh. So sorry." She stood to exit. But when she got outside, all the street signs started to seem familiar and she couldn't remember which way was back to his apartment.

She started walking in one direction, but that took her what appeared to be the wrong way and farther away from campus, so she turned around. But that didn't seem right either. When she finally decided to give up and turn her phone back on, a man approached her.

"Hey sweetheart. How's about sharing some of what's you got wit' me?" He wrapped his arm around her, pulling her against his side.

She quickly maneuvered herself away and discreetly pulled her phone out.

"Hey! Where you going?!" He caught her in his grasp again. "I have what you like."

"No. Please don't touch me again. Just leave me alone," she ordered, pushing him away, causing the man (who wasn't too much bigger than her) to stumble.

She walked faster to get away from him, but he followed behind her, harassing.

"Don't you be like that, now. I like that body you got there. I'm gonna watch you from a distance and then I'm gonna sneak attack!" His pestering continued. But Melanie texted James.

S.O.S

Then she turned her phone to vibrate and slipped it into her pocket as the man took her arm and pulled her into an alley directly behind them, shoving her against a wall. He restrained her arms overhead, and Melanie's breathing deepened as she began to cry.

"Please let me go. I don't know what you want. I don't have any money..." she begged.

He laughed in her face. "I don't want your money, sweetheart. I want your lovin'," he said as he held her face and licked her cheek, kissing down her neck, pushing Melanie's face to the side, scrunching it against the wall. Thinking quickly, she raised her knee, catching him right in the groin, causing him to crouch down protectively, giving Melanie a chance to run.

"Help! Someone! I'm being attacked!" she yelled as she emerged from the alley, but no one even looked in her direction, as the people around continued going about their business with earbuds in, walking past with their phones against their faces, engaged in conversation, oblivious to the world.

She quickly hurried down the next street, watching behind herself as she pulled her phone out and texted James again, when the man ran up behind her, yanking her into an empty parking lot behind another business.

James!! Help me!!

But the man quickly had her phone from her hands, inspecting it carefully.

"Who's this you're talking to?" he asked as he looked at the texts. "Jamie? Hm... Nope." He tossed it to the ground. Stepping on it. "Jamie's not as much of a man as me." He reached in and tried to lick her face once more, but she was crying heavily now, and she spit at him.

"What do you think you're doing? You're not playing nicely," he said to her, wiping his face, then moving his hands to lift up her shirt.

But Melanie's fear was relieved as she saw James approaching. As he tiptoed up behind the man, he motioned with a "shushing" motion of his finger over his lips for Melanie to stay quiet and not give his presence away, and he quickly seized the man from behind, turning him around, and tossing him against the brick wall to have a good look at him.

"That's right, you puny ass mother fucker. You messed with the wrong girl!" James threatened, holding the scrawny man up by his throat against the wall to mimic what he'd done to Melanie, and James watched his eyes grow worried as he looked James in the face. "You keep your hands off my girlfriend or the street sweeper will be dusting you up on Monday morning. Understand?"

He nodded, and James said, "You apologize to her!"

"Sorry," he nodded.

James tossed him down, moving Melanie aside, then he knelt down and whispered, "You're lucky I don't kill you," into the man's ear, holding his face with a firm grip, pressing the man's chest down with his knee. "Consider this the luckiest day of your life. Had you done anything worse, you'd have lost your life!" Then James stood, shoved his boot down onto the man's face, picked up Melanie's broken phone, tossing it at him, before he took Melanie's arm, leading her out to the truck.

He helped her in and once he was in on his side, he angrily looked to her.

"Where in the hell have you been? Why were you all the way over here? I've been getting your voicemail for hours!!" he screamed at her.

"How did you know where I was?" she asked, not looking at him.

"I put the location service on your phone so I would always know where you are. Once you turned on your phone and sent me a text, I found you easily. This isn't a good neighborhood. College students are morons. Now I'm glad I did it because I love you, Mel."

"Oh. Well, thanks, I guess," she smiled at his over-protectiveness. "I'm sorry, by the way."

Tears rolled out of her eyes and down her face and she just rested her head on the window as he drove away.

"Are you okay? Did he do anything to you?" he asked a few minutes later.

"I'm fine. He didn't hurt me. I just feel panicked."

"Why were you over here? Why didn't you just get coffee near the campus?" he asked, frustrated, but more worried than angry.

"I saw a woman in the medical library today," she responded.

"Melanie..."

"Who is she, James?" she whipped her head around angrily.

"Who is who? There are *thousands* of students here," he snapped back, tossing his hands out questioningly, feeling aggravated at her jealousy.

"Well, she knew *me*."

He turned his head in her direction as he pulled into his designated parking spot, thinking on her comment for a moment. "Why are you so upset about a girl in the library who knows me that knows *of* you? Maybe I told a lab partner about you. I don't know."

"James... she *saw* a picture of me," she accused before storming out of the truck and up the stairs into his second-floor apartment, with him hurriedly following behind.

"Melanie? So what? I don't understand what that shows about anything? Why are you so upset?"

Ignoring his question, she stomped into the bathroom to get cleaned up, feeling disgusting and violated from that man's mouth and hands being all over her.

But upon her return to the hallway, James was still standing there waiting for an explanation. "I'm not dropping this. I want to know why you're upset about that girl."

Fury overtook her, and she busted into the bedroom where she snatched up the picture of her off his nightstand.

"This is why!" she yelled, "You told me you didn't have any girls here when you were here those weeks before break without me! You lied! Everything has been a lie!"

"No! I didn't lie. There were no girls here!" he defended.

"She has red hair too, which I now know means the 'poster story' you fed me was bull shit too! What else has been a lie, James?"

"Why are you behaving like this? I didn't lie to you! I have your picture on my phone, on my computer, and in my wallet! That girl could've seen it anywhere! My poster is right there!" He pointed to the bedroom wall to his right, "And you know I have one at home too!"

She turned away from him, crossing her arms, gripping her necklace.

"Mel, what's got you so upset?" he asked, walking over to comfort her.

"Who is she? Did you sleep with her ever?"

"Why does it matter? You're the only one for me now. You know that. I love you." He moved closer, reaching his arms out to her. But she pulled away, turning to face him.

"Because you're obviously still talking to her. And I saw what she studies; she's in medicine. It's not like you have class with her. You must be going out of your way to interact with this girl."

"No! I swear it isn't like that. A redhead in medicine?" He thought about it for a moment before he responded, "She works at the bar..."

"Ugh!!!" she spewed angrily, "What is it with you and redheaded waitresses, James?!" She stomped out of the room.

Hurrying after her, he said, "I don't like her, Melanie. It was my first year here. Willis and I were just looking for fun.

Melanie?" He walked over to where she was standing, trying once again in a useless effort to comfort her. "Babe, why are you so upset? You know I love you. I can't help what I did before I knew you. But you need to know I'm faithful to you now. Are you upset about that guy tonight? Want me to kill him?" He smiled. "Because I will. I'll pound that mother fu..."

"No!" She spun around to look at him, tears pouring from her eyes.

"What's the matter?" he asked.

"Just go away!" she screamed.

"No. Not until you tell me what it is you want from me. I need to know what it is you need. I don't know what else to do for you. What do you want from me?!" he asked, obviously frustrated.

"I need more than this!" she screamed.

"More than this... What?!" he yelled back.

"I want to know that you're going to be here for me," she sniffled, stepping away, wiping her eyes. "Or I can't be with you anymore."

"Be here for you? I'm here right now, aren't I? I'm a jerk. I know I am, and I did stupid jerk things before I met you. I can't change that now. But I want to do whatever it's going to take to make this work." He stepped closer and wrapped his arms around her. "I love you. What's it going to take?"

"Tell me you love me," she replied.

"I love you, Melanie. I do." He hugged her tighter.

"Marry me." She sighed.

"What?" He pulled away to look in her eyes, surprised by her words.

"I'm pregnant again, James."

"Hell, I've got some strong soldiers," he joked.

"Why don't you want to marry me?" she asked, ignoring his humor.

"I do."

"Then what are you waiting for?" she shrugged.

"The right time."

TEN

Graduation was nearing and Melanie's baby bump was growing, but James wasn't quite ready to give up his partying days, because each weekend as Melanie stayed home feeling sick and sleepy, James went to his local favorite to get drunk with Willis.

"You're going out again?" she asked, as he threw on a shirt and gelled his hair.

"Just with Willis," he said, walking over to kiss her goodnight.

"I was hoping you'd stay with me. Whenever you get back from a night out with your friend, you're passed out and..."

"I won't be long. I promise." He kissed her cheek, then her tummy, and headed for the door.

"James?" she asked, "Is this because of that pretty waitress?"

"Oh Mel." He walked back over to her. "Absolutely not. You're the one for me. Well, you and this little one." He knelt down and kissed her tummy again.

"Just don't forget about us while you're getting drunk tonight and you're checking out that fiery redhead." She moved away from him and walked away into the bedroom, closing and locking the door behind her.

James sighed, running his hands through his hair, contemplating on whether he should be going out with Willis or staying home. But he decided that Melanie's hormones were probably just taking over in her and she would sleep it off, so he walked out and hopped in the truck, driving down the street to the bar, but he sent her a text on his way there.

Mel, I love you. Call me if you need anything. I'll be home early.

"What can I get you this evening?" the pretty, green-eyed, redhaired waitress asked James, as he sat around with Willis and some other friends.

"Beer," Willis answered.

"Rum and coke," Andrew, a younger guy Willis met in class, responded.

"How about you, James?" she asked. "You want that whiskey sour?"

"Not tonight," he replied.

"No?" she asked.

"Just bring me a Pepsi and lemon. I need to be home at a decent hour."

"James!" Willis shouted. "Going soft on us?"

"No. I just know my priorities, guys. I can't stay long."

"Why? Gotta get home to the little lady?" Andrew teased.

"As a matter of fact, yes. I do. There's a beautiful woman waiting for me," James said.

"Well, then why don't you man up and *show* that woman who's boss?" Andrew laughed.

"Don't man," Willis cautioned.

"Have you ever even *had* a woman?" James asked Andrew.

"I've had my share of fun," Andrew said, "But dating isn't my scene. I like to play the field. Keep my options open."

"Is that so?" James responded, thinking that Andrew's comment reminded him of himself not too long ago.

"Hell yeah! I could take home any girl in this bar! Your woman included, if she was here."

James pounded his fists on the table, standing up, lunging forward at Andrew.

But Willis was right there to calm James's flaring temper. "James, think of Melanie. You don't want to get arrested for a bar fight. It would ruin everything and tarnish your clean record. But also, who would be there for her? Now, you know Melanie only wants you."

"What's wrong, James?" Andrew continued provoking after James sat back down. "Worried that your woman might have a go at a *real* man? Feeling like she might like that thought there, James? Feeling nervous about the little lady and how faithful she is to you? Well, why don't I give her a call? What's your little honey's name? Or should I ask... what would she want *me* to call her?"

"Forget it, Willis. I'm bustin' this guy up," James said as he stood and walked around the table.

"I ought to beat the hell out of you!" James yelled to Andrew, holding him up against the wall of the bar by his chest, ready to release his right hook.

"I was only playing around! Do I detect a sensitive side to someone?" Andrew mocked as he moved his arm up to give James a punch to the gut. "I wonder if maybe your woman has *already* had a go with another man!"

"Okay boys, here you go. Enjoy!" The waitress said, returning with their drinks, but looking to James as he held Andrew up against the wall, ready to give him a beating. "James," she said, "You need to take a breather."

"Yeah, James. We all know that *she* was your first choice," Andrew said, pointing to the red-headed waitress, just as Melanie walked in and witnessed the whole scene.

James saw the mortified look on Melanie's face, so he released that right hook, laying Andrew down with a strong blow to the face.

"I *knew* I remembered her face," the waitress said to Willis as she watched Melanie run over to James, as he reached down to get in another punch.

"What do you mean?" Willis asked.

"I saw her in the library one day and asked her about James because he comes in here all the time, but he seemed especially down one night last fall, and I knew it had to be about a girl. A downtrodden face like the one he was wearing could've only been because of a girl. Well, he showed me the picture on his phone of that beauty." She pointed to Melanie.

"Oh," Willis said, now understanding that Melanie was confused about things.

"Jamie!" Melanie screamed as she ran up to him.

Andrew held his bleeding face and spit at James, "You stupid redneck honky! Go back where you came from!"

Melanie gasped at Andrew's words, knowing that it was going to enrage James. But he looked to Melanie standing there, hands on her hips, worry on her face, and he stood up.

"I may be a southern redneck honky with a funny accent, but I'm *not* stupid. I don't need to prove my intelligence to *you.* But I know how you're here and what you're studying. But me? I earned my way here, and I know my roots. Watch yourself or you'll be sayin' hello to the floor again." He walked away from Andrew and over to Melanie, gripping her shoulders in his hands.

"Melanie? Why are you here?" he asked, pulling her in close.

"Let's just go," she started, as she turned to walk out, not stopping until she reached the truck.

He got in on his side of the truck, looking over to her angry face. "Are you angry?" he asked, though already knowing the answer.

"I'm a mixture of emotions that you don't want to experience right now. Let's just go," she replied.

He drove back to the apartment and stayed silent the whole drive back but looked her way several times wanting to say something, feeling distressed at her tears.

"Why were you there?" he finally asked as they stepped into the apartment.

"I don't like that you go to that bar, James. Knowing that you've had previous relationships with these waitresses but still go back there, it makes me so uncomfortable. Why do you need that?"

"I don't. It's just a place I like. It's not about the girl," he explained.

"Is this why you don't want to get married?" she asked.

"No."

"I'm going to take a shower," she said, as she walked down the hall and into the bathroom.

Desperately wanting to join her in there, he used the excuse of washing his bloody hands, which were beat up from punching Andrew.

"Mel, it's me. Just washing the blood off my hands," he said, locking the door and looking to her naked silhouette in the shower behind the curtain, admiring her pregnant shape, desiring her badly.

He decided to slip off his own clothes, and he glanced around the curtain to see her sudsing up her body with a loofa. He let out a satisfied moan at the sight and climbed in, closing the curtain behind himself.

"Jamie!" she exclaimed, as he wrapped his arms around her from behind, softly kissing the curve of her neck.

"I couldn't resist. You looked so tempting." He continued kissing her, turning her to face him.

"Well, even if I'm angry with you, I always want you." She reached up to hold his face in her hands, planting some kisses on his lips, but they were interrupted by a steady pound on the door.

"I didn't know I was going to be sharing an apartment with the love connection! I'm moving out!" Willis hollered in to them.

Melanie pulled away, giggling, but James yelled back, "Don't be jealous because you're not getting any! Now go away, because *I* am!"

He took the loofa from her hands and started running it up and down her back, enjoying every moment of seeing her that way, but she suggested, "Let's go to our room."

He quickly hopped out of the shower and grabbed a towel for her and one for him, then they raced across the hall to their bedroom.

"I hope Willis didn't just see that!" she said with a giggle.

"Nah, but who cares?" he shrugged.

"Um, I bet *you* will when he's commenting about me to you over your bowls of cereal tomorrow morning," she winked.

"I'll lay that hick right out onto that tile kitchen floor," he threatened humorously.

"Jamie!" she said, as he tackled her playfully onto their bed.

"I love you," he said, as he kissed around her earlobe and moved to her lips. He paused briefly, looking in her eyes, contemplating something he wanted to say.

"What is it?" she held his cheek in her hand, stroking his nose with her thumb as he hovered over her.

"Melanie... I..."

"Jamie, you're making me nervous. What do you want to say?"

He shook his head. "Nothing. It's not the right time." He resumed kissing her, switching positions, and they disappeared under the sheets.

"Shut... Up..." he complained, as he pounded the alarm, trying to hit the snooze and make the obnoxious noise stop.

He sat up and slid into his boxers, and walked out to the bathroom, trying not to wake Melanie. After jumping in the shower and brushing his teeth, he returned to the bedroom to dress for the day, where he did a quick toss on of a t-shirt and a pair of jeans, and then some fingers through his hair, and he felt he was ready to grab a bowl of cereal and head to class for his long day.

"Melanie," he kissed her forehead to tell her goodbye. "Mel," he tried once more, when he noticed...

"Oh my god!!! Look at all the blood!!! Willis!!! Call 911!!!"

Willis rushed into the room, as James continued trying to wake Melanie.

"Holy Jez... What the fu... What happened to her?" Willis asked, looking at the blood-soaked sheets underneath Melanie.

"Hell if I know! Call the fuckin' squad!" he yelled as he leaned her up and saw the blood pooled underneath her back.

"Oh my god," he breathed as his heart dropped to his stomach and he looked at her bluish colored face, and he tried to feel for her pulse to be sure she was alive.

"Melanie, baby. Stay with me," he panicked and reached to feel her slow but steady pulse. "Oh! Thank the stars."

"They're on the way, James," Willis said, walking back in, coughing uncomfortably at Melanie's naked body. "Um... maybe... we should get her a shirt? You got one in here, man?" Willis pointed to the closet.

"Jeez! Shit! You erase that from your memory!" James said, as he pulled to cover Melanie with the sheet.

"Done," he handed James a plaid button down from the closet and turned away while James moved her flopping arms into it, one at a time.

"Melanie," James cried. "Wake up. Why won't you wake up?" He held her unconscious body against his, as he anxiously awaited.

James remembered being taken to church as a young boy by his grandparents, and he decided that he'd put those lessons to use at this moment and pray...

"If there's a God out there somewhere, please listen to me. I know I'm not deserving of anything and this woman deserves better than what I am, but don't punish her because of me. I'll make it up to her. I swear I will. Save her and I'll make amends. I need her. I'll do anything."

"She's in here," Willis said, leading the paramedics into the bedroom."

"Finally," James said at the sight of their entrance. "She won't wake up. I found her like this. She's 24 weeks pregnant," James explained.

"You're the husband?" the paramedic asked.

"Uh, no. I'm her boyfriend, but..."

"Who's her decision maker?" the paramedic asked, as they lifted her onto the gurney.

James held back his anger at the sound of an all-too-familiar question that he didn't like being faced with again.

"This is *my* baby too!" he yelled.

"The state of Connecticut doesn't allow boyfriends to make decisions on girlfriends or their babies. I'm sorry. You need to alert her family. We're taking her to Yale-New Haven Emergency." They exited with her down the stairs.

"What the hell was that?" James said to Willis as he rushed out the door.

"I don't know," Willis said.

"Lori? Hi. It's James," he said as he dialed Melanie's mom and climbed into his truck to follow after the squad.

"There was a 19 year old young woman brought in by a squad a few minutes ago," James said as he rushed up to the triage desk upon entering the ER entrance of the hospital.

"Name?" the clerk asked.

"Melanie Crosby."

"Family or friend?" she asked.

"Neither," he replied.

The woman looked up to him, confused. So, he clarified.

"She's my girlfriend. I'm the father of her baby."

"Ohhhh. One of *those...* I'm sorry, but only family members are allowed in right now. There's a doctor's note in the file right here."

"No! I need to be in there! She could be dying!!" he yelled and gained the attention of everyone in the surrounding vicinity. "Can't you talk to someone?"

"I'm sorry, but you'll have to wait for a family member to arrive. Please take a seat over there." She pointed to the waiting area by the triage desk.

James balled his fists up at his sides and clenched his jaw, trying his hardest not to explode on the impossible woman in front of him as he backed away and moved to sit in a chair.

After a few minutes of relaxing his elbows on his knees, cradling his head in his hands, and running his fingers frustratedly through his hair, he called Lori.

"*Hi James,*" she answered. "*How is she? How's our peanut?*"

"I haven't got a clue. They refused to let me see her because I'm not family. These damn Yankees," he said.

"*You're serious?! She's in there alone? No! My baby!*"

"I'm fixin' to call my Mom and sue this hospital," he replied.

"*Don't kill anyone, now. I'm about ten minutes away. I'll be there soon to get it sorted out,*" she responded before hanging up.

James dialed Janice immediately.

"Mom, it's Melanie," James said.

"*I know. Willis called Kaylee, who called Amber, who called me,*" Janice answered.

"I'm surrounded by meddlers!" he shouted.

"*How is she? How's our little one? Tell me it isn't the puddin' pie?*" Janice asked.

"Mom, they won't let me see her! I have no idea what's going on!"

"*What do you mean they won't let you see her?!*" Janice asked.

"Well, the squad picked her up and took her away, saying that because I'm just the boyfriend, that I can't see her or make decisions for her, that I have to wait for a family member," he sighed.

"*Well, son. I guess this means it's decision making time,*" Janice said.

"What?" he asked.

"*You know exactly what I mean. I have to go. Call me when you know something. Love ya, baby boy.*"

"Bye Mom."

Lori walked in a few minutes later and went directly to the same clerk, with James immediately rushing to her side.

"Hello again." The clerk looked to James. "And you are?" she asked Lori.

"I'm here to see Melanie Crosby. I'm her mother."

"She's in ER room number five. Through those doors right there," the clerk answered and pointed to the doors behind her.

"He'll be joining," Lori said.

The clerk nodded, acknowledging.

"Why couldn't I get through just 20 minutes ago?" James asked.

"Be an immediate relative or a spouse and you can." The clerk motioned for them to enter.

His heart was pounding through the wall of his chest the whole time from the concern about the state of Melanie, and he watched the numbers on the doors as they walked through the ER hall.

"8... 7... 6..." he said to himself as they hurried to approach her door.

"Hello. You're the mother?" the young female doctor said to Lori as they entered the room.

"Yes. Lori Davis. This is..." She began to introduce James, but the doctor interrupted.

"I need to speak with you about her condition. Privately."

"Doctor, you may speak right here. This is her boyfriend and he is the father of her child. Whatever you have to say concerns him too," Lori insisted.

"Yes, of course."

James breathed a sigh of relief that Lori was going to defend his rights with Melanie, but he still felt troubled that he had no defense against the system when it came to Melanie or their baby.

"Melanie has a condition called Placental Abruption. It means that the baby's placenta has detached from the uterine wall and is causing her to bleed out. Her blood count is severely low and she needs a transfusion, but we fear that she is too early to deliver. Currently, your baby is alive and is stable. If we can stop the bleeding for a little while and keep *Melanie's* condition stable, then we might be able to save the pregnancy. But if we deliver now, then the baby might be too early."

"What will happen to Melanie?" James asked.

"Either way, she's going to need blood. How much and how long she'll take to recover depends on how long we try to prolong the pregnancy," she explained.

"You said the baby *might* be too early," Lori asked.

"Yes. Sometimes babies at 24 weeks survive in NICU. Sometimes they don't."

James started pacing the room looking at Melanie's pale face, as she laid on the bed slipping away from him, and he continued to listen to Lori debate over whether or not to save Melanie now or later based on a theory that the baby may or may not live at 24 weeks. Frustrated, he finally said, "DO I have a say in this?"

"Yes, James, of course you do," Lori answered.

"I don't want to take the chance of losing the woman I love because there *might* be a chance that the baby could survive. If we know that giving her blood now, *today*, is going to save her life. Then why in the *hell* are we standing here wasting time?! Go! Do it!!" he demanded.

"Okay." Lori agreed. "If that's what you want."

The doctor nodded, walking out of the room. A few minutes later, she brought back papers for Lori to sign. And James walked away to sit next to Melanie's bedside thinking that he had big decisions to make.

"The surgery will take about 45 minutes," the doctor said, as a hospital tech wheeled Melanie away, prepping her along the way. "I will update as soon as we are able. A nurse will take you to the surgical waiting area."

"Do you think she's going to hate me?" James asked Lori about 30 minutes later as they sat in surgery waiting.

"Why would she? You did what needed to be done to save her life," she replied.

"Yes, but I probably killed our baby," he said, hanging his head in shame.

"Sometimes the best decisions are the hardest decisions to make, James. That doesn't mean they don't need to be made," she replied. "She'll love you all the same."

Melanie woke several hours later after receiving the transfusion, only to be greeted with the devastating news that her baby did not survive the delivery. Having lost so much blood in-utero, the pregnancy had suffered too many complications and did not recover. Naturally, she was devastated.

"Just the nurse, dear. I need to switch out your meds," her nurse said upon entering the hospital room the next day.

"It's me too," James said, stepping inside. But Melanie didn't turn to look at him, upset over his actions the previous day.

He sat next to her on the bed and patiently waited for the nurse to finish. Once she exited, he said, "Melanie, I know you're upset about the baby. I am too. But I need you to consider things from my perspective. You were dying. What would you do if I was dying? Would you just let me?"

"No," she responded.

"Then can you try to understand this, even just for a moment?" he asked.

She shifted her position as he helped her sit up. And he continued, "I couldn't just watch you die. As the man who loves you, I had to do something. I'm always going to be here for you. I promise. I felt like I needed to protect you. I'll always protect you because I love you. Please try to forgive me. My actions were only out of the deepest love in my heart."

"I suppose I'm just feeling a loss from the baby. This is number two now," she said, looking up to his face.

"I'm sad too, Mel. That was my baby girl too. Please forgive me," he said.

"There's nothing to forgive," she said, motioning for him to hug her. "We'll get through this. I know it. I love you, James. As much as you love me, that's my love for you."

"What would you have wanted to name her?" he asked.

"Oh, um..." she thought about it for a moment but couldn't think of anything, when he finally said, "Annie."

"That's my middle name," Melanie said.

"Yeah. I would've named her Anne, but we could've called her Annie because there's no one in the whole world I want her to be like more than her mother. You're the strongest woman I've ever known."

ELEVEN

"I'm so excited!" Melanie squealed as he exited the auditorium after graduating with distinction and summa cum laude.

Janice and Bruce were right there congratulating him too, along with Willis, who graduated with a degree in Chemical Engineering.

"All that studying and hard work has finally paid off!" Bruce said, hugging his son and Willis.

"Come here, my baby," Janice moved Bruce and took her son, tightly wrapping her arms around him. "I'm so proud of you! Now, we need to go and celebrate!"

"Congratulations Willis! How does it feel?" Bruce asked.

"I pretty much feel the same. What about you, James?" Willis said.

"I feel like a nap," James shrugged.

"No way!" Janice said. "We are celebrating!"

"Yes!" Melanie exclaimed. "Where to? Jamie, you guys choose!"

"Uh, you know? I'm not really hungry," he said.

"We will not take no for an answer!" Janice said.

"Really, Mom. It's been a long day," he replied.

"Jamie, your parents just paid for all these years of school for you. You should let them take you out for some dinner," Melanie insisted. "Willis! Say something!"

"Me? I'm innocent here."

Kaylee nudged him to cooperate and he said, "I'd like a good steak because if I don't, I won't be getting any dessert."

"Jeez Will..." James shook his head, and Willis smirked while he wrapped his arm around Kaylee, just to piss off James.

"Now, how about it, Jamie?" Melanie asked.

"Fine," he complained. "Just let me take my gown off. Mel, meet me at the truck in a few minutes." He walked away toward to parking lot.

"Alright," Melanie said as he walked away.

"Willis? Where's your Aunt? Will she be joining?" Janice asked.

"Nah. Her health isn't so good. She couldn't make it. But it's all good. I'm happy to be here with my first family." He reached out and hugged Janice, then he headed for Kaylee's car.

"Melanie, is James upset about something?" Janice asked.

"I haven't got a clue," Melanie answered, watching him walk away.

"Maybe it's because," Willis began, but Kaylee elbowed him in the gut, quieting him.

"Because what?" Melanie asked. "Willis," she took a few steps towards him, pointing her finger in his face, "Willis! What do you know?"

Kaylee shook her head at him, so he sealed up his lips like a zipper with his fingers, and Melanie let out a sigh of exasperation.

"Well, we'll meet you at that steakhouse he likes. Alright?" Janice said.

"Yeah..." Melanie acknowledged, walking away to their truck.

"James..." she said, climbing in.

"Hey," he extended his arm to pull her up. "Where are we headed?"

"To that steakhouse you like. Is that alright?"

"Of course."

He backed out of the lot and stayed silent for a few minutes until Melanie said, "What does Willis know?"

"What does he know... what?"

"He knows something about why you're upset. I want to know what it is."

"Hell if I know," he answered.

"I know you're lying, James. I know you better than *you* know you."

He looked over to her, shrugged, and then kept quiet the whole way to the restaurant.

"Table for seven, please," Bruce said as they arrived and the hostess seated them around a large table in the back of the restaurant and everyone began looking over the menus as she took drink orders, but Bruce asked the question James was dreading.

"Son, have you started the search for jobs? Are you coming back to Atlanta? I'm sure the engineering department with my airline could use you. Want me to give them a ring? Has no one reached out to you? Why haven't you said anything to us? Has he said anything to you, Melanie? What's he been discussing with you?"

"Actually, he hasn't really said anything to me. I have no idea at all," Melanie replied, looking curiously at James.

"Dad, I'd rather not discuss this here. It's between me and Melanie, if you don't mind," James responded.

"Alright, then... Willis! What are *you* doing with that degree?" Bruce asked.

"Um," Willis hesitated, looking to Kaylee and then to James and finally to Melanie.

Melanie looked around the table at everyone, nervously wondering what the big secret was, and her curiosity was deepening about why James hadn't talked to her about where they were moving, if not back to Atlanta.

"What's going on, everyone? Why can't I know what's going on? James? Kaylee? Willis? C'mon... out with it!"

"Melanie, it's not the time," Kaylee said, causing Melanie to look worriedly at James.

Amber whispered, "Don't worry. I'm sure he just has something wonderful planned that he wants to surprise you with at just the right moment. You know Jamie."

Melanie was trying to feel reassured, but in her heart she knew that James was keeping something from her.

"I don't know," she replied and glanced over to James.

"Well, let's just be glad he's done with school! Now you can come home," Amber said.

"Let's hope." Melanie sighed and turned to sip her sweet tea, letting her mind wander to endless possibilities of "what ifs" and "maybes."

The waitress came bouncing over to take their orders. "What'll it be tonight, folks?"

"Porterhouse for me," James said.

"How would you like that cooked?"

"Rare." He shut his menu and handed it to her.

"I'll have the T-bone," Willis said. "Rare for me too."

The waitress continued taking orders, but Melanie whispered to James, "Please talk to me. I'm really worried. Why does everyone else know what's going on but I don't?"

He moved his hand down to hold hers where it rested on her lap and he said, "Everyone else doesn't know. Mom doesn't know. Dad doesn't know. Amber doesn't."

She yanked her hand out of his and crossed her arms over her chest, looking away.

"And for you, honey?" the waitress asked Melanie, finally making her way back around.

Melanie looked to James. "No, thank you. Nothing for me tonight." She closed her menu, handing it to the waitress.

"Melanie, you're not eating?" James whispered.

"No," she answered, shaking her head. "I don't have an appetite."

"This is about me not telling you; isn't it? I know it is because I know how stubborn you can be."

"Well then you'll know that lecturing me over it won't do any good." She turned away, sipping her tea.

He looked to the waitress just as she turned to leave and said, "She'll have the roasted chicken with a salad and a potato."

Melanie snapped her head around to rebuke him, saying, "How dare you!"

"I can be just as stubborn," he countered. He grabbed up his Pepsi and lemon, taking a drink, proudly declaring his victory.

A few minutes went by and he'd talked to Willis about some nonsense or other, and she decided to excuse herself to the restroom to compose her thoughts.

"Excuse me for a few minutes. I need to disappear," she said, moving away from the table and to the back of the restaurant into the restrooms.

"Is Melanie alright?" Janice asked.

"Of course she is," James responded. "Why would you say that?"

"Well, it was the *way* she said that, is all. Just concerned for her."

After washing off her face, and taking a few deep breaths, she looked to herself in the mirror and said, "He loves you."

"Hi, Melanie," a man said to her on her way back out.

"Nick?!" Melanie exclaimed, surprised to see him there. "What are you doing here in Connecticut?"

"I have a conference here in New Haven. I'm in for the week." He looked down the aisle and noticed Janice sitting with her husband, "I assume it would be too presumptuous of me to think that you might want to join me for dinner again. I mean, as long as I'm in town."

"Well, actually..."

"Hello, Mr. fancy-suit lawyer. Were you just hitting on my girlfriend?" James asked, as he approached from around the corner, coming out of the men's room.

"Wha...uh..." Nick stumbled over his words, while Melanie stared nervously at James.

"Look," James held his finger in Nick's face. "I *should* give you a proper goodbye. But, I won't because you're a colleague of my mother's, and in order to be decent to *her* I will let you walk away."

"Was that a threat?" he replied.

"It was *more* than a threat," James responded, bracing his hand against Nick's chest.

"Ever heard of disturbing the peace?" Nick warned.

"C'mon, Jamie," Melanie begged, pulling on his arm.

He nodded to Melanie, giving in to her, backing away from Nick.

"Stay away from my girlfriend," he threatened. Then he pulled Melanie along back to their seats.

"Where were you guys?" Amber asked.

"Ran into one of your work colleagues," James said to Janice.

"Oh?" she responded, knowing by the look on James's face that it wasn't a good confrontation.

"Yeah," Melanie sighed.

"*Oh*," Amber said. "I bet it was that pretty-boy lawyer you went out once, wasn't it?"

Melanie shook her head to Amber, asking her to stop, but Amber continued.

"Look, Jamie. I don't know why you're so jealous. So what Melanie went out with *one* other guy?! You've been out on dozens of other dates! In high school you were always going out with girls! I think Melanie should get her share too! Stop being so controlling."

"This isn't really a conversation that's headed in a direction I think we should continue," he said, looking to Melanie, who was obviously upset.

"Don't listen to Amber," he whispered, "It wasn't that many girls, and I didn't sleep with them, not back then."

"I'm not upset about that!" she spat.

"Then what?" he asked.

"You were coming to check up on me!"

"Yeah? So?" he said.

"You don't trust me!" she accused.

"No. It's not that at all. I was just..."

"I'm not going to run off with another man, James. If anything was ever going to make me leave, it certainly wouldn't be another man! You are just so impossible sometimes!" She turned away, sipping on her tea again.

"Melanie, I was worried for you," he added before the waitress brought their food, setting the plate he ordered for her down in front of her. She watched as James dug into his gigantic steak, and her growling stomach wanted to do the same to the delicious chicken staring her in the face, but her stubbornness wouldn't allow it. So, she just sat sipping her tea.

"You know," he whispered a few minutes later, "Eating the food I ordered for you is just like saying, 'Thanks, James. I love you and I know I can be stubborn sometimes, but I know that *you* love and care for me.' However, it won't make me think any less of you. If anything, I'll think more of you because I'll know you appreciated it."

She smiled slightly and took a bite.

"So, we'll see you in Atlanta soon?" Janice said to Melanie as they were leaving.

Melanie shrugged. "I hope."

Later that night, Melanie started packing her things in the bedroom to prepare for their move next week, when she found a letter from the Department of the Air Force.

"*Dear Mr. James Hunter,*

We are pleased to inform you of your acceptance into the United States Air Force Officer Training..."

Her breath escaped her as she dropped the letter onto the bedroom floor and fell to her knees, allowing the overwhelming shock of the letter to break her heart.

"Melanie?" James said, walking into the bedroom, seeing her kneeling on the floor with the letter next to her and her face in her hands.

She looked to up to him. "When were you going to tell me?!"

"I... uh..." he replied, and stumbled over his words.

"This isn't something you keep from the woman you love! This is a decision we make together!" she yelled, as she stood, holding up the letter.

"It's the best way for me to get to NASA," he explained.

"But it's not the best way to get to me." She pushed past him and started gathering her things, tossing them into a suitcase.

"Mel, it's not like I'm gonna be going to war or anything. I'm an engineer. I'll be checking plane designs, testing prototypes and things like that. It's not going to be like what you think."

"When I lost the baby a few weeks ago and nearly lost my life, you promised that you were always going to be here for me. Now I don't know what to believe! I can't even trust you not to keep secrets from me!" she yelled.

"I *will* be here for you. Training is only several weeks. I'll be back before you know it, baby. I promise." He held her shoulders in his hands, forcing her to face him.

"When are you going to marry me, James? When will I be your priority?" She grabbed her bag and walked out.

"Melanie? Where are you going? Are you leaving?" He rushed after her.

"Yes, James. I'm leaving. I want you to be committed to *me* for once. I need to know that you're going to be here for me! You care about your career, your planes, and everything else, but I never know if I'm going to have a future with you!" she yelled as she walked to the door and took out her phone.

"Hi, Daddy."

FOUR WEEKS LATER

"Sugar! There's a letter for you!" Greg hollered as he walked into the living room and handed Melanie a letter. "That's the fifth one this week. Why don't you write him back?" he suggested.

"I can't, Daddy. I need to move on. James isn't interested in a family. He doesn't want the things in life that I want."

"I understand. At least send him a letter to let him know that you want him to stop. This is... well, I don't even know what this is." Greg shook his head, walking away.

"Desperate," Melanie said. "He just wants sex when he gets back," she mumbled under her breath and then rolled her eyes and opened the letter.

Melanie,

I know I've screwed up so many times that we can't begin to count it. But, I promise I'll amend. I'll be everything you ever wanted and more. Not having you these last few weeks has made me realize how much I need you in my life. Never before had I ever wanted to be tied down to someone or something, and I thought that I wanted it to just be me my whole life. But then you came. You threw my heart into a mess and I didn't know what to do anymore. I was so confused. But now I'm not. I'm not confused anymore and you need to know it. I know what I want now. I want you, Mel. Forever. I know it. I'll do whatever it takes. I swear. I'm a fool for you. I've fallen hard. I love you.

Always,

James

After letting herself cry for a few moments over his beautiful words, she considered that he might actually be telling the truth. But then she remembered the last time he went away, and how he'd begged to get her back, yet nothing changed. She wiped her eyes, folded up the paper, and tucked it into the pile with the others.

TWELVE

"Are you sure she's coming?" James asked as he sat at the bar, whiskey in hand, nervously anticipating Melanie's arrival.

"Kaylee and Amber promised, man. She'll be here. Just be patient," Willis said, slapping James on the back and taking a drink of his beer. "Why don't you just have another whiskey and practice what you're going to say?"

"Yeah," James agreed. "You're right." He downed his whiskey and cradled his face in his hands, thinking of the perfect thing to say.

"Practice on me," Willis said.

"No," James refused.

"C'mon, man. Propose to me, lover," Willis waved his hand for James to get down on his knee.

"It's not going to happen. Now shut up and let me think!" James yelled as he opened the ring box, staring at the two carat, radiant cut diamond on a raised platinum setting, wondering if she was going to like it, or if she would even accept it.

"Let me help," Willis stood and walked behind James, coughing in order to get his attention. "I've got inspiration."

James turned around to yell at him once more, but was stopped when he watched Melanie walk in with Kaylee and Amber, sitting down in the far corner booth, looking more beautiful than an angel, in a tight fighting, off the shoulder, red dress that hit just above her knees, with her brown hair curled and draping over her bare shoulders.

"Will, I'm falling in love all over again, man," James said as he watched Melanie sit down.

"I know, buddy. Cupid's hit you hard. We'll let them get settled and then I'll go through with the plan. Alright?"

He nodded and downed another whiskey.

A few minutes later, Willis stood and walked over to Kaylee, whispering in her ear. She took his hand and followed him to the far back end of the bar where the pool tables were.

James nervously downed another whiskey.

A few minutes later, Kaylee appeared to the booth where Amber sat with Melanie. She whispered something to Amber, and then they disappeared to the corner with the pool tables together, leaving Melanie confused and alone.

James downed another whiskey before he slipped the ring box into his pocket and walked up to the booth.

"Hi, Mel," he said.

"James," she responded.

"Waiting for someone?" he asked.

"I'm here with Kaylee and Amber, but they're... well, actually..." She looked around, "I don't know where they went. What's up?"

"May I sit with you?" he asked, pointing to the empty booth.

"James..." she hesitated.

"Please?" he persisted.

She nodded.

"You are really beautiful tonight," he said, widening his eyes.

"You're always complimenting me," she blushed, resting her elbow on the table, hiding her face in her hand.

"I mean it. When I saw you walk in, you were more beautiful than the first time I saw you, if that is possible. And it is. You know why?"

She looked up to him, "Why, James?"

"Because I'm madly in love with you. It doesn't matter what struggles come our way. Nothing is going to change that for me. I want you and I want us. I want you and me for always. It's you, Mel. You're the one. I'm sure of it. I've been going out-of-my-mind crazy these past weeks without you. I'll do anything. I'll prove it." He stood and held out his hand and Willis ran over to the juke box, turning on a song, as James led her to the dancing floor, holding her in his arms, gently swaying back and forth, singing the words to Carrie Underwood's song in her ear...

"I would bet my life like I bet my heart, that you were the one, baby. I've never been so sure of anything before, you're driving my heart crazy. I can't hold out; I can't hold back now, like I've done before. Darling, look at me. I've fallen like a fool for you. Darling, can't you see? I'd do anything you want me to. I tell myself I'm in too deep; then I fall a little farther, every time you look at me..." and he held her firmly against his chest while she sang...

"How do you do that, babe? Make me feel like I'm the only girl alive for you. I don't know what it is that makes me fall like this. First time in your arms, I knew. The way you held me, I knew that this could be what I've been waiting to find..."

And as the song continued and they kept dancing, he whispered, "I love you, Melanie. Will you marry me?" which wasn't the grand speech he'd been planning to give, but it seemed so perfect, and it was the perfect time.

Unsure of what to say, completely surprised by his question, she stayed quiet and kept dancing, gripping his shirt, holding him close, just happy to have him in her arms again and have her head against his strong chest. But she moved away as the song ended, so he pulled out the ring as he knelt down on one knee in front of her, not paying attention to anything or anyone else in the whole world except her.

"Melanie Crosby, I love you, and I want to spend the rest of my days showing you that. Will you marry me?" He opened the ring box and as soon as she saw the ring and realized that he meant the words he was saying, she beamed with excitement.

"Oh my god! Jamie!" she exclaimed. "Yes! Of course I will!" She held her hand out for the ring. Radiating with complete happiness, she stared at the gorgeous beauty of a ring on her finger as he hugged her, twirling her around, and Amber, Kaylee, and Willis rushed over to congratulate them.

"Oh guys!" Amber squealed. "I'm a bridesmaid!"

Melanie nodded, happily complying.

"Let's see it!" Kaylee shrieked excitedly.

Melanie held out her hand to show off her big rock, and Amber complimented him for a job well done.

"Big brother, you *actually* did a good job! Did Mom pick this out? Because this is gorgeous! I have a hard time believing you picked this out," she sassed.

"Shut up, Amber," he said, "I picked it out. Alright?"

"I love it, Jamie. You did a great job," Melanie admired the ring for a moment, before taking ahold of his face and whispering in his ear, "How about a reunion tonight? It's been a while and I'm missing you like crazy."

His eyes and ears perked up at the mention of that and he said, "Alright ya'll. It's been a great night. But..." He grasped Melanie's hand and quickly led her out of that bar and to his truck.

"You know..." she said when they got outside.

"What?" he asked, helping her up into the truck.

"A long while ago you promised me two truck sessions, which you have yet to deliver."

He rushed around to his side of the truck, hopping inside, and hurrying to start the truck. Looking to her as he drove away, he said, "As I said before, you've got yourself a very irresistible deal." Then he hurried to his favorite quiet place under the big the willow tree near bridge overlooking the pond.

"Melanie?" he asked as he was removing her dress, kissing down her neck.

"Hm?" she mumbled back, pulling his face up to kiss her lips, sliding down underneath him on his black leather seat, allowing him to collapse on top of her.

Moving up momentarily to pull off his own shirt, he asked, "Why didn't you return any of my letters? I wrote you one nearly every day. It was tearing me apart."

Savoring having him in her hands again, she ran them along his bare chest and up his back as she answered, "It was too hard." Then she pulled him back down to kiss her again and began working on his pants buckle.

Then he mumbled in between kisses, "So... you... did... miss me?"

Taking his face firmly in her hands, and forcing him to look her in the eyes. She replied with more conviction than she'd ever said anything in her life, "I missed you every day. When you're not here, it hurts. You're like a part of me now. Losing you was like losing the babies. Don't you ever leave me again, James Hunter."

Gently caressing his hands up and down her back, he promised, "I'll always be here for you. I'm going to love you until my very last breath."

Her heart was satisfied and she knew, as he gave in to his passion, that it was no longer lust which motivated him but it was love now, and she was happy.

THREE WEEKS LATER

"He'll be here, sweetie. Don't you worry," Amber said as she fixed up Melanie's hair into a beautiful French twist with delicately placed curls at the top.

"I'm not so sure," Melanie replied, fighting back her tears.

"Look at me," Amber said. "That man loves you!"

"I know. But he doesn't want a wife." Melanie stood and walked up the back stairs of the banquet hall to exit the back doors to the gravel lot.

"Melanie?" Kaylee asked as she saw Melanie walk past where she was standing smoking a cigarette. "Where are you going?" she hollered, tossing her cigarette down, going after her.

When Melanie started running towards her car, Kaylee got out her cell and dialed Janice. "Mom! Melanie is running to her car! I think she is leaving! I think we have a real emergency here!"

"*Why? Aren't you trying to stop her?*" Janice asked.

"Well, she's still in her casuals and I'm in a dress and heels! What are ya expecting me to do?" Kaylee hung up the phone and dialed Willis.

"*Hey sweetness,*" Willis answered.

"Shut up. I don't have time for you. Where's your lover?"

"*Ouch, my sweets. That's quite a way to greet your hot chocolate. He just grabbed his dress mess blues from their house and he's heading over to the banquet hall to get changed. I'm headed that way soon. I just picked...*"

"SHH! You talk too much! I just wanted to know what *he* was doing! I don't care what *you're* doing!" She hung up.

"Melanie!!" Kaylee yelled, waving, as she ran over, just as Melanie was starting her car.

"What is it?" Melanie asked, rolling down her window.

"Where are you going, honey?" Kaylee asked.

She shrugged in reply.

"The wedding is *that* way," Kaylee pointed to James's favorite spot on the bridge over the pond. "Do you need socks for those cold feet?"

"I'm not the one with cold feet, Kaylee. You should talk to your brother about that."

"Melanie, sweetie. Jamie doesn't have cold feet. He's on his way here right now. Now, c'mon out of that car and get your buns back in that hall to get yourself dressed." Kaylee pulled the door open, yanking her out.

"No, Kaylee. Just leave me!" Melanie fought back.

"Nu uh. I won't. You're not running out on my brother. Get your ass in there!" She pulled Melanie along and back to the banquet hall.

"He doesn't want to get married!" Melanie argued as Kaylee practically dragged her inside.

"Yes, he does! Willis said he's on his way here right now. He already got his uniform. What makes you think he doesn't?" Kaylee asked, sitting down next to her on the chairs in the banquet hall.

"Last night, I heard him talking to Willis."

"What did he say?" Kaylee questioned.

"He said something about..."

"I said that I only proposed in order to win her back," James said from behind Kaylee, causing Melanie to sniffle and wipe her tears. She looked up to where he was standing and was awed at the handsome sight of him in his full dress blues.

"You look... wow," she said, motioning at him.

He walked over to her, and motioned for Kaylee to leave, then he sat down where Kaylee had been seated, taking Melanie's hand.

"Melanie, what's going on?" he asked. "I hear you're about to run out on me." He leaned in, holding her face, and softly kissed her cheek.

She sniffled again. "You said..."

"I did what I needed to do. I *knew* that you wanted to get married, but I was being immature and just didn't want to take the leap, I suppose. But I knew that's what you'd been waiting for from me. Even though I wasn't ready, it doesn't mean that I don't *want* to marry you. It only means that I needed to grow up. So, I stepped up my game and used the proposal as my means of winning your heart again by letting you know I was kicking it up a notch. I'm a freaking genius, in a way. Now, you get your pretty ass downstairs and put on whatever dress my sister conned you into buying. Because I know you're going to be gorgeous. Plus, it's bad luck to see the bride before the wedding." He kissed her cheek once more and slapped her rear as she skipped away.

James nervously waited outside in the far lining of the trees where it met the edge of the grass, as the park workers set up the chairs for the guests to arrive.

"You okay, man?" Willis asked, as he watched James pace the grassy knoll next to the bridge.

James looked over to the area where his mother was standing, ordering all of the flowers to be put out along the aisle where the white chairs had been set up in grassy area next to the gravel lot.

"The bouquets go there, not there!" Janice hollered to the workers, as she pointed for the bouquets of crème roses and white lilies accented with purple statice and green pitta negra to be strategically placed on each aisle. Melanie had chosen those particular flowers in order to enhance the blue of James's evening attire uniform.

"I'm good," James finally responded after turning his attention away from his distracting mother, "Just worried about Melanie."

Willis slapped his hand on James's shoulder. "She loves you, buddy. She'll be here."

The guests started to take their seats, and James stood to the side by the trees until the military preacher gave him the "OK" to make his way to the front by the beautiful trellis archway perfectly placed in front of the bridge, which had also been draped with the arrangement of flowers Melanie had picked out.

The hired pianist and cellist duo began to play a beautiful rendition of "All of Me" by John Legend and Amber walked down in a swirled lavender and cream gown, accompanied by Willis, who was also in his formal blues, followed by the flower girl— James's cousin— who tossed crème rose petals onto the grass. Then Melanie walked up to the end of the aisle, stopping at the end while everyone stood and turned to face her and James's breath escaped him as he saw her in an off the shoulder, bell-bottom, satin dress, with a long, full veil, holding a bouquet of crème roses, white Asiatic lilies, and white miniature carnations.

Everyone was entranced by her as she nervously took each step to the front, keeping her eyes focused on James every time her heels hit the ground.

She reached the front and he mouthed, "You are so beautiful," and he took her hand, turning to face the preacher, where they stood in front of the same bridge they visited on night they'd met.

And the military preacher began the wedding ceremony.

"Good Evening, everyone. James and Melanie have chosen this location for their wedding because this is where they shared their first date and also their first kiss. It is a day that they hold close to their hearts and want it to remain in their memories as a most joyous place for all of their days. To all of you, many of whom they have known for quite a number of years, and have shared in their good memories, their special moments, or even their sad times, they wanted you to also be a part of a place that they hold so dear. Thank you all for being here to celebrate in their love with them and being a part of a once-in-a-lifetime moment with them.

We look to Janice and Bruce, James's parents here in the front row on the left. And also Melanie's mother, Lori, and her father, Greg, and the bride and groom would like to extend a special thank you for all that their parents have done for them over the years. Let us begin...

A marriage is a commitment and union of two individuals and though it is voluntary, it is a decision decided entirely with one's whole mind and heart. We are about to enter into that union.

James, do you come here freely and without reservation to give yourself to Melanie in marriage? If so, answer 'I do'."

"I do."

"Melanie, do you come here freely and without reservation to give yourself to James in marriage? If so, answer 'I do'."

"I do."

Melanie's eyes began to tear up as James couldn't resist mouthing, "I love you," to her as the preacher continued.

"Now that we have made your intention to become husband and wife known, let us continue with your vows."

"James and Melanie have chosen to write their own vows." He looked to James, then said, "James please begin."

"Melanie, my whole life had been planned out in my mind and I thought I had everything figured out. I had this image of what I thought was perfection and nothing was going to stand in the way of that. However, sometimes there are plans that are greater than our own or else I wouldn't be here today. When you showed up, I was given a new image of perfection and I'm so grateful for you. Because of that, I promise to be there for you in everything. I will build our dreams together and uplift you through times of trouble. I will celebrate with you in times of happiness but be there through grief and sorrow. I promise to give you respect, love, and loyalty, no matter what comes our way. I will not fail you, Melanie. I will love you until my very last breath."

Melanie took a deep breath, as tears streamed out of her eyes, staring at James, never thinking he'd utter those words to her.

The preacher turned to her.

"Melanie, your vows."

"James, falling in love was something that was new and challenging for me. But the person you are made the adventure of love unique and special and I can't wait to spend the rest of my life with you. Being your wife is an honor that I will cherish and hold dear for all of my days and I will love, respect, and care for you for as long as I live. James Tyler, I will be there to dance with you in all of our joys, triumphs, and celebrations, but I will also cry in your arms at every sadness, broken dream, and failure. With all of my heart, all of my soul, and all that is in me, I promise this day forward, until my very last breath."

Happiness crossed James's face as she said those words, and the preacher said, "The rings please..."

Willis leaned forward, handing James the rings.

The preacher said, "These rings are an outward sign of the inward love you share for each other and the bond which already unites you and the two hearts that are in love. Wear them proudly. James, place the ring on Melanie's finger and repeat after me..."

"With this ring, I thee wed. As this ring is a circle and has no end, so my love for you will have no end; my love is also forever."

Melanie looked down to the gold ring on her finger and smiled widely, until the preacher said,

"Melanie, place the ring on James's finger and repeat after me..."

"With this ring, I thee wed. As this ring is a circle and has no end, so my love for you will have no end; my love is also forever."

"Let the rings you exchanged today always remind you of the love you share for one another."

James and Melanie grasped hands tightly knowing that they were about to be presented as husband and wife.

"My wish for newlyweds is that your lives together be blessed with a lifetime of love and that you always remember and keep the vows that you declared in front of each other and your friends and family here today. Bless this new marriage with a kiss."

"Gladly," James said as he took Melanie a bit more eagerly than he should've and kissed her a little bit more passionately than considered appropriate for a wedding, stirring commotion from the guests. But James never cared what anyone thought, except Melanie, of course.

Melanie whispered, "James."

He pulled away and the preacher announced, "I present to you, Lieutenant & Mrs. James Hunter. Welcome to the Air Force, Ma'am."

Releasing her arms from around his neck, she took ahold of his hand, Amber handed her flowers back to her, and they faced forward to the crowd of people, who stood and clapped, congratulating the happy new couple.

James hurried down the aisle tightly gripping ahold of Melanie's hand, pausing at the end to plant another passionate kiss on her lips.

"This is it," he said pulling away, as the guests moved by, congratulating them on their way to the banquet hall a few hundred yards away up the hill.

"What is?" she asked.

"The beginning," he smiled before pulling her in for another. "I'm starting over with you, Mel. I'm hitting reset, right here, right now. You're no longer Melanie Crosby. You're Melanie Hunter now, and that means I get a reset button. Okay?"

Smiling widely, she nodded, "Okay."

THIRTEEN

"We present to you, Lieutenant and Mrs. James Hunter!" Willis shouted into the microphone as James and Melanie entered the reception hall hand-in-hand.

All the guests stood, clapping and cheering, while James enthusiastically entered, arms extended overhead, as Willis motioned for the DJ to turn on the music.

"What this world needs is a few more rednecks..." The Charlie's Daniel's Band played from the speakers, and Melanie turned to scold Willis while James shouted out in excitement.

"Time to get drunk!" James yelled out, as the song only egged him on.

"Hell yeah!" Willis joined in on the excitement, as Kaylee looked to Melanie apologetically.

"Break out the booze, rednecks!" James shouted. But just as he was moving to join his friend at the bar, Melanie pulled his face down to whisper in his ear. "Remember, if you get too wasted, we won't get to enjoy the first night of our honeymoon." Then she kissed his cheek and his earlobe, nibbling on it slightly, causing a sigh to escape from him.

"I'll be *plenty* ready for tonight. The question is... will *you* be ready for this hick?" He winked and walked away to the open bar.

She shook her head, allowing her mind to drift into a fantasy world about him, watching his every move as he removed his jacket, tossing it over an empty chair, and she saw that he'd *altered* his uniform wear a bit and that the back of his white dress shirt was redone in a blue fabric with fighter jets. She laughed as she saw that Willis had touched his up in

157

a similar manner, but in a deep red color marked with beer bottles.

"DO you see those two?!" Kaylee said walking up, humored at the sight of them.

Melanie laughed. "Yes. They look... I don't even know. What are we going to do with them?"

Sighing, shaking her head, as she watched them clank their beers together and chug them down, Kaylee replied, "I have no idea. But you're the crazy girl who married one of them! At least I know where to draw the line." She nudged Melanie with her arm, but Melanie just stared admiringly at James as he grabbed a whiskey and walked up to some of his other Air Force buddies.

"So, where's the honeymoon?" Kaylee asked.

"I have no idea," Melanie replied, slightly frustrated, but mostly excited.

"What do you mean you have no idea?!"

"We are staying somewhere here in Atlanta tonight and then flying somewhere tomorrow. But he won't tell me where."

"How odd," Kaylee remarked.

"The mother of the groom is kindly requesting that each guest makes their way to their designated seats. James, she means you!" the DJ announced.

"You can tell the mother of the groom that this is *my* wedding and I'll get drunk when I want, and I'll eat when I want!" James looked over to Janice and then to Melanie, who was now walking his way.

"The groom is hereby refusing dinner, claiming the time now is for drunkenness!" the DJ declared, causing the guests to erupt into laughter. "Here comes the bride. Let's see what she has to say to this!"

"James, come and sit down!" she ordered, grabbing his hand. "You're not even drunk yet. What's with you?"

"Nothing, babe. Just having a little fun," he turned away and faced Willis once more.

"Hey," she said, pulling on his hand.

"Yeah?" he responded, still facing away from her, paying attention to the commotion going on with Willis and his friends.

"James," she tugged on the back of his shirt.

"What?" he spun around to see her upset and composed himself.

"What's going on? Your mom wants everyone seated for the food. The caterer is ready. I'm feeling nervous. Is this, James—the man who never wanted a wife in his life— starting to realize that he's married and is feeling smothered and choked by that ring on his finger?" She walked away before he could answer.

"Melanie!" he called for her as she walked to the table, but she didn't look back.

Sighing heavily, he ran his hands over his face and walked up to the DJ, asking for a small change in plans as the caterer began serving dinner.

"The groom has requested a song while the caterer begins. Since it's his reception, I couldn't possibly deny him. So, if I could get the bride up here. Your husband requests your presence, please."

"What are you doing?" Melanie asked as she approached the dance floor, where James was waiting with a sweet smile on his face, apologetically holding out his hand for her.

The DJ switched on "All of Me" by John Legend, and James led her to dance.

"Dance with me, my wife," he said.

They swayed, moving back and forth in a slow circle with his arm extended out, hand-in-hand, intertwining his fingers in hers, and the other wrapped protectively around her, pulling her against him with his hand tightly gripping her back, as she laid her head against his chest, and curving the other arm around his to rest her hand on top of his shoulder, clutching his shirt in her palm, holding onto her everything.

"Melanie," he whispered, "I'm not afraid."

She glanced up at him, so he continued, "I *want* this ring on my finger. The man in me has changed. I'm not the same man I used to be. I'm ready for a family, but I'm only ready for a family with you. I want you and I want us, forever. With all of my heart, I am ready for this." He leaned down and kissed her, and she stretched her arms to embrace around his neck.

"I've wanted that ring around your finger since the day I raced down the stairs and saw you drive away for Yale without me," she said.

"I didn't know you followed after me," he responded and smiled slightly.

"My heart broke at the sight of you leaving. I don't want you to leave me ever again. Promise you won't ever leave me again."

"I promise I'll do my best. I love you, Melanie. I don't want to be away from you any more than you want to be away from me." He pulled her up to kiss him as the song ended and the guests clapped softly, and James and Melanie pulled away from their passionate kiss, remembering they were in front of a crowd of over 200 people.

"Let's eat," he said, taking her hand and leading her to sit at a table with Amber, Kaylee and Willis, and their parents. "What are we having? I don't remember deciding on a menu," he asked once they'd taken their seats.

"Your mom and I didn't let you decide. We knew you'd choose steak or fried chicken." She teased.

"What else is there?"

"Why don't you just wait for your plate? Look, here it comes." She pointed to the servers bringing the plates to their table.

"Congratulations on your special day," the server said as she laid the plates down in front of them, then moving on to Willis.

"Thank you," Melanie replied, as the server moved past and James looked over to her.

"Really, Melanie?" he whispered to her.

"Just eat it and be grateful that you're married to me. If you don't complain, I'll do that *thing* you like, tonight."

His eyes widened, producing a small smile, and he asked, "You promise?"

She nodded playfully, "I swear. Now eat your salmon and behave yourself."

He blew her a kiss and turned to eat, but he looked to Willis, who had chicken that was covered in a mushroom sauce.

"How did he get chicken and I have this healthy shit?"

"Because I don't *get* those special privileges like you do to make me behave," Willis joked, glancing over to Melanie.

"And you *never* will!" James snapped. "Now shut up and eat your man food, while I eat my girlie food."

Melanie gigged at their banter, leaning in to say, "Don't worry. You're the only one I'd ever give special privileges to, *especially* that makes him behave." She nibbled on his earlobe, releasing a small sigh from him as he frustratedly dug his fork into the salmon.

A little while later as everyone was finishing their plates, Amber approached the DJ asking for a cordless microphone, then quickly hurried over to the elegant wedding cake that Janice had ordered, which was white and four tiered, with crème and blue roses and lilies descending in a curve from the top to the bottom.

"Time for the cake! Get over here, you two!" she called out.

Melanie quickly grabbed up his hand and raced over to Amber, where she was holding out a knife for them to cut their slice.

"You know, Jamie," Melanie whispered as they placed their hands on the knife together over the cake.

"What's that?" he asked.

"You said you get a restart?"

"That's right," he said.

"Here's the chance to put that to the test," she said, pushing down the knife, then grabbing the server, pulling out their piece.

She took a small portion on her fingers and he took some on his, grinning slightly, and she was certain she was getting creamed with it.

However, to her beautiful pleasure, he delicately fed her a piece and he leaned in, kissing her, sucking the icing off her lips, whispering, "Only good things for us now, Mel. You are my wife. You won't regret me."

She placed his piece on his lips and he kissed on her fingers for a few moments before she leaned in, tasting the leftover icing on his lips, whispering back, "I could never regret you. You're everything I've ever wanted."

"I am?" he asked.

"How could you not know that?" she asked, just staring into his eyes for a moment, as Janice approached, ordering the cake to be served by one of the workers.

"I suppose I've just messed up so many times over the time we've been together that I'm just hoping to become..."

She held her finger to his lips, shaking her head. "No. This is the reset, remember?"

"Yeah." He kissed her finger.

"Okay! Let's get the bride and groom out to the center of the dance floor!" the DJ hollered, and Amber brought Melanie her bouquet to toss, and Willis sat in a chair nearby, stirring excitement in James because he knew what that chair was for.

"Okay, all you single ladies!" Amber yelled out. "It's time for the bouquet toss. Scatter 'round over here. Mel, you go over there!" She pointed next to the chair where Willis was currently seated, and Melanie headed over as the ladies scurried over to catch the throwing bouquet.

James positioned himself right in front of her, trying to help her aim for Kaylee.

"Throw it with all your strength, a little to the left, so you can reach Kaylee and freak out Willis," he whispered in her ear, stirring a smile.

"Heh, okay," Melanie agreed.

With all she had in herself, she reached down, hurling that bunch of flowers as far back and to the left as she could, smacking Kaylee right in the face.

"You were supposed to catch it, Kaylee!" Melanie yelled when she saw what happened and heard all the laughter.

"No! I'm not marrying Willis! Now, everyone move along with the festivities. Show's over!" Kaylee hollered.

"What's the matter with you, man?" Willis reprimanded, slapping James on the back of the head as he walked past. "Now she's gonna be getting ideas of marital bliss in her head and all that junk."

"Do right by my sister or you have to deal with me," James retorted, "You're already lucky I haven't already put your ass six feet under!"

"Go ahead and try!" Willis provoked, walking to take the microphone from Amber.

"Okay, now men. Your turn. Melanie, you sit yourself in that chair right there, and..." Willis said, but James walked up.

"I'll take it from here, Will, thanks," James interrupted, hurrying over to the bar.

"A whiskey," he asked, as Willis had the DJ turn on a song...

"Love is like a bomb, baby, c'mon get it on..." and James danced his way over to Melanie, smashing his shot glass on the floor as he approached.

"Pour some sugar on me..." he said with a wide grin, kneeling down, lifting her dress up over his head, disappearing underneath.

Commotion and laughter erupted from all the guests as they watched James completely disappear under her dress, with only his legs and feet showing, not returning back out right away.

However, Melanie began to feel shy at James's display and tried putting an end to it.

"James Tyler! Get out of there!" She laughed, tickling his sides with her toes as he removed her garter with his teeth, kissing her inner thighs on his way out.

He finally emerged, victoriously, head held high, fists in the air, garter between his teeth.

"Give it up for James Hunter, everybody!" Willis proclaimed as the guests laughed, clapping, along with Melanie, as she adored her spirited husband and his crazy antics.

"More of that to come later," he leaned in, whispering.

By the end of the evening, Melanie was exhausted, and after their final dance together she whispered, "I'm ready for time alone. Just me and you."

"Me too. Let's get out of here. I have somewhere special for us to be."

They made the rounds of saying goodbye to all the guests, stopping to his mother and father, and hers last.

"You take good care of each other, okay?" Janice said hugging them as they exited. "And don't be strangers. We are going to..."

James interrupted her with a quick shake of his head, and Janice put her finger up to her mouth shushing herself, understanding.

"She's yours now," Greg said, shaking his hand. "I'll admit that you surprised me, James. But, you pulled through and now I'm counting on you to take good care of her."

Looking to Melanie, James reassured, "You can count on it. I won't let either of you down."

"So, husband... When are you going to tell me where we are going?" she asked, eagerly anticipating their arrival as they drove across Atlanta towards the neighborhood where his mother and father lived.

"I'm just going to show you. Close your eyes," he said.

"What? You mean, like close them right now?" she asked as he pulled into a small neighborhood.

"Now."

She obeyed, noticing the truck pulling to a standstill, and even though she wanted to know what was going on, there was a part of her that loved the mystery and secrecy.

She heard him coming around to her side, opening her door.

"Give me your hand, but keep your eyes closed."

"What's the big surprise?" she asked as he helped her down out of the truck.

"Just come," he answered, pulling her along holding one hand over her eyes so she wouldn't peek.

"When?!"

"Now!" he uncovered her eyes, letting her see that she was standing in front of a two story, tan house, trimmed with white, with a red front door, and a white letter "H" hanging on the front.

"Jamie?" she asked, stepping closer. "What is this?"

"Ours."

Quickly turning to face him, she stumbled over what to say, "Wha... how?"

"I bought us a house. Welcome home." He held up the key. "Go in. Take a look around." He motioned to the door.

An excited squeal escaped from her as she leapt into his arms, kissing all over his face.

"I can't believe you! How did you manage this?!"

"I have my resources," he replied, carrying her to the door.

"Your mom put that 'H' on the door. I know it wasn't you," she teased, as he put her down and walked inside.

"That is true. I did have some help with the furnishings." He pointed around to all the furniture and went into the living room.

"James," she called for him, as he started walking the open floorplan house, while she stood in the entryway near the stairs. "You're going the wrong way," she flirted.

Stopping immediately where he stood, he started unbuttoning his shirt as quickly as his fingers would move, tossing it to the floor. Then he hurried over to where she stood at the stairs.

"I was coming back. Believe me," he said, moving his hands to rest on her hips and his lips to her jawline.

"I just thought you might need a little coaxing." She reached around and started unbuttoning the fasteners to her gown, but he stopped her and began undoing them himself.

"Really, Mel? When have I *ever* needed coaxing?" He kissed down her neck but stopped to say, "What the hell is wrong with these clasps?! Are these husband proof?"

She laughed, and offered, "Let me help," getting them unfastened quickly, having her dress off her shoulders and to the floor in no time, satisfying his eyes with her left in only the skimpy undergarments.

"Mmm. If I would have known only *this* was hiding underneath that dress all evening, I would have brought you home so much sooner. You're a tease. Let's get you upstairs and make you officially my wife." He picked her up and moved quickly up the stairs to their bedroom.

"Welcome home, Mrs. Hunter," he said, laying her down on their bed.

FOURTEEN

"Welcome to Crete. We hope your stay is very much to your liking. Please let us know if there is anything you will need," the concierge said as he escorted them to their room upon arrival.

"This place is so beautiful!" Melanie said as they walked into their room which overlooked the sea. "I never thought you were going to do it!"

"What's that?" he asked, wrapping his arms around her where she stood looking out the window.

"I never thought you would fly for me." She turned to face him. "I especially never thought you'd fly me to our honeymoon destination." Reaching up to kiss him, she added, "It's so romantic, Jamie. You are so special, one of a kind. I love you so much."

"I love you too. Now, what should we do today?"

She yawned, "Nap. I'm so sleepy."

"You want to go to bed?" He raced over to the bed, tossing off his shirt and unbuckling his pants on the way. "I'm ready for you, baby."

"Jamie! Is that all you ever think about?" she giggled.

He shrugged playfully. "Maybe. But take it as a compliment. At least I'm thinking about it with you." Then he climbed under the covers. "Come on, Mrs. Hunter. Your husband awaits."

She quickly joined him, slipping underneath the covers from the bottom of the bed, tickling his legs as she crawled on top of him, enjoying his laughs the whole way to his lips.

"James." She shook him, trying to wake him from his snoring slumber. "James!"

"No." He smacked at her.

"Jamie!" she pushed at him again. "Wake up!"

"Go away, woman! I'm trying to sleep!"

"No! I want some food. Order me some room service."

He looked over to her. Then he reached beside the bed and picked up the menu. "Order whatever you want. Charge it to the room, babe. Now, let me sleep. Love you."

"Ugh!" she spewed, realizing she'd been defeated.

She browsed the menu for a few minutes and picked up the phone.

"I'd like room service for room 331. I want the spinach and feta egg wrap, with potatoes, and a coffee."

"Hey," James interrupted, "Let me in on that."

Melanie smiled. "I'll also need an order of sausage with scrambled eggs and toast, with an orange juice."

"Thanks, babe." He blew her a kiss, cuddling up beside her as she hung up the phone.

"I thought you wanted to sleep?" she asked.

"Well, I knew when your food came if I tried to steal a bite, that my chances of having sex later would greatly diminish," he admitted.

"Already very wise in the ways of marriage and still so young. I think you're going to make an excellent husband, James Hunter." She pulled the blankets over them, disappearing underneath, until there was a knock at the door at the arrival of their food.

"Room service!" the man called from the door.

"We'd better get that," she whispered.

"I don't want to. I like where we are. Let's just stay here forever. Please?" he begged.

Kissing down the front of his chest, she said, "James... Tyler... I ... want... my...food!" then she hopped up and threw on the hotel provided robe and ran to the door.

"*Kalimera,*" the man said as he looked Melanie up and down, obviously checking her out.

James took notice, and he rushed to slip on his boxers, hurrying to the door beside her, making his claim.

"Here's your tip. Move along there, waiter man," James said signing the receipt, handing him 5 euros.

"What was that?" Melanie asked as they walked in to eat at the breakfast table in the room next over.

"Just letting him know what's mine."

"What?" she opened her tray, taking a sniff, enjoying the scent. "Mmm..."

"That guy was checking you out," James said.

"Oh? I didn't notice. But, so what? It's not like he gets me. I only want you." She leaned over and kissed his cheek, "Jamie, I married you for a reason. I picked you. Out of all the world and all of the men, I wanted *you.* Remember that. Now, eat up. I'm keeping you busy for the whole week we are here. Understand?"

"You're my whole world, Melanie. You know what I want to do?"

"Hm?" she mumbled as the feta cheese fell from her mouth while she chewed.

"I want to stay locked up in this room, showing you just that."

"Well, you'll have plenty of time for that. But, I want to go cliff jumping!"

He laughed. "What?!"

"Yeah! I heard someone talking about it in the lobby. I want to try it! C'mon, Jamie!" she said excitedly.

"Melanie, No."

"What? Why?" she whined.

"It's too dangerous. I've almost lost you twice. Now you're finally my wife and it's my job to protect you and keep you safe. I'm going to do just that."

She looked up to him, held his face in her hands, and said, "I think that's the most beautiful thing you've ever said to me."

"Now come over here where it's safe," he moved her over to his lap and moved the robe off her shoulders just slightly, laying soft kisses on her shoulders as he said, "Stay right here in my arms."

"I think I will stay right here... forever." She leaned against his chest and kissed him, but then added, "Really, Jamie. What do you want to do today?"

"How about we start with the beach? I reserved two umbrella chairs. It should be beautiful down there today."

"Sounds perfect."

"Finish eating and then change into your suit. I'm going to jump in the shower and wash up." He took one last big bite before he walked away. "Hey." He turned back, glancing over his shoulder.

"Hm?" she looked up as she stood and cleaned up their mess to put it at the door for the housekeeping.

"I love you with all there is of me. I just want you to know that."

"I know it." She smiled and skipped away to put on her swimsuit.

After digging through her suitcase for her *actual* swimsuit, she realized that Amber had switched up a few of her essentials, and instead of her cute, red, retro one-piece, Amber packed her a skimpy, blue bikini.

"Amber!" she chastised as she put the halter top bikini on and tied the bottom ribbons on each side.

"What the hell is that?!" James yelled out at the sight of her very skimpy bikini.

"Amber..." Melanie rolled her eyes.

"You're not wearing that thing. Put something else on."

"James, I don't *have* anything else. Amber helped me pack. She switched out my swimsuit for this one." She shrugged.

"You're kidding! I don't want all of those men out on that beach gawking at my wife. You look... Mmm! Amazing. But you're for me only," he said.

"Don't be jealous. Honestly, I'm flattered. But..."

"I know, I know. I'm being too husbandly?" he asked.

"No. You can't ever be too husbandly. Husbandly is a good thing."

"Then, what am I being? Too... controlling?" he asked.

"No. Not the right word," she disagreed, pondering her thoughts and his.

"Intense?" he continued searching.

She nodded. "Yes. That's it. You're being too intense. Just calm down and know that I love you. I don't want anyone else. Remember when we first met and I was so worried about all those other women you'd been with and how worried I was all the time?"

"Yeah."

"Well, that's you right now, except without any justifiable reason because you're the only man I've ever wanted, James. Ever," she explained.

"I'm trying. I just know I married up."

"Oh really? Because I was thinking the same." She looked down to his hand as she lightly played with his fingers. Then she looked back up and said, "Let me just grab a beach towel and we'll head down. Put your shorts on. Okay? You think I'm going to attract gawkers? Go out there in that towel and see what happens." She winked at him, yanking off the towel as she skipped away.

"Can I get you anything to drink?" the beachside waitress asked James as he laid on the beach lounge admiring Melanie floating in the waves.

"No. Nothing for me. But that pretty girl out there will have a lemon seltzer."

"Is that your wife?" she asked.

"It is," he replied.

"She's a lucky girl."

"I'm the lucky one," he looked up to the waitress, who was clearly flirting with him, and continued, "She's the best thing to ever happen to my life."

"I see. How's someone get a guy like you?" she asked, winking.

"Are you asking how I met my wife?"

"I'm asking in general."

Knowing she was trying to flirt with him, being very experienced in the field of women before Melanie, he only said, "My wife won my heart because she is a beautiful person inside and out."

"Well, if it ever turns sour..."

"If *what* ever turns sour?" Melanie asked, grabbing her towel, giving him a kiss, sitting next to him on his lounger.

"Nothing. I got you a lemon seltzer," he said, as the waitress walked away.

She situated herself between his legs, leaning back against his chest, and asked again. "If *what* ever went sour, Jamie? Was she talking about us? Were you flirting with her?"

"No. I wasn't. She *was* talking about us, but I wasn't the one doing the flirting, babe. I swear." He hugged her tighter.

"Oh. So, she was flirting with *you?*" she asked.

"Yes. But I'm not going to be like that anymore. I'm not going to lose your trust. Please believe me," he said.

"I do. Let's just promise that we'll always be honest and trust each other, okay?" she asked.

"Fine by me."

"Come for a swim with me?" she asked, taking his hand, pulling him off the lounger.

"Sure."

They hurried down to the water and he scooped her up, running into the waves with her arms and legs wrapped around him.

"How did I get so lucky?" she asked as he held her in the water, waves splashing against them.

"It wasn't luck. It was fate. I reached for the stars," he said. "You're my heaven."

They spent the rest of the day enjoying the beach, splashing in the water, soaking up the sun, and loving each other. Every minute he had, he used to admire how beautiful she was, but she did the same to him, and both of them truly felt they couldn't be any more in love than they were in those moments.

That evening, he arranged for them to have dinner on their balcony overlooking the sea.

"What would you like to do tomorrow?" she asked just as they finished eating and they were watching the setting sun.

"Don't you worry for tomorrow, my beauty. Tomorrow is already planned."

"Oh?" she wondered.

"Just wait and see." He walked away to the shower, and when she saw what he was doing, she quickly followed behind to give him an after-dinner treat.

The next morning, *he* woke *her*, for a change.

"Mel!" he said, brushing the slobbery strands of hair away from her face. "Wake up."

"No. Go away." She pushed at him.

"C'mon. I have a surprise for you."

He persisted in waking her until she gave in, and then he hurried into the shower and got himself ready for the day. After which, he kept her waiting in anticipation until they arrived to their destination.

"An airplane? What are we doing?" she asked as they approached the small commuter plane.

"Everything you need will be inside," the pilot said, opening the rear door to the plane, helping Melanie inside, while she looked confusedly back to James, as he followed in behind her.

"Come on up. I'm your instructor," the fit, dark haired man said as he handed her the suit and backpack. "I'll be jumping with you today."

"Jumping?!" Melanie exclaimed, as she heard the roar of the plane engines and she watched the man help James securely fasten his pack and put on goggles.

"You wanted to go diving. Well, I figured the safest way to satisfy that was to let you jump out of an airplane. There was no way I was letting you jump near any sharp and jagged cliffs. But, I'm trained to jump out of airplanes." He grinned at her.

"You're out of your mind!" she squealed.

"Maybe, but I'm enjoying every minute of it, and I'm loving every second of it with the woman I love."

"I'm so excited!" she exclaimed.

"Good," he said, "That was my plan."

The instructor went over their procedures and safety instructions and readied them to jump.

"Alright," the instructor said, opening the door. "We're almost there. I'm going to count to ten, and then jump. Ready?"

"When do I open my chute?" Melanie asked.

"One... Two..." the instructor began.

"When do I open my chute?" she asked again.

"Just watch me," James said as the instructor said "ten," and James yanked her out of that plane and they went freefalling into the sky together.

"Ah!" she screamed. "This is amazing!"

"I knew you'd love it!" he hollered back as the wind smacked them in their faces, while they fell faster and faster.

"When do I open my chute?" she asked again. "Everything's getting closer, Jamie!"

"Not yet!"

They fell through the air for a few more minutes until he finally gave her the signal, and she pulled her chord, releasing the parachute, giving her a little tug upward before they slowly floated to the ground.

When she bumped onto the grass butt first, he looked to her, laughing and said, "You were supposed to land with your feet!"

"That's a lot harder than it looks!" she grumped, face scrunched at his laughter.

"I managed." He extended his hand down to pull her up and helped her unfasten her parachute. "Did you like that?"

"Like it? I loved it! Let's do it again!" she exclaimed.

He chuckled and reached to unhook his own parachute and said, "No. Once is enough, my little daredevil. Now I'm ready to take you back for other extracurriculars."

The week in Greece passed quickly, and after snorkeling, swimming with sea turtles, and scuba diving, they were soon headed home, and James had to resume his duties at the base where he worked as an aerospace engineer, testing prototypes, analyzing the designs of planes and missiles, and fixing issues with malfunctioning fighter jets.

"I'm worried for you," Melanie said one morning as he dressed in his long sleeve blues.

"No need to be worried. I'm mostly at a computer all day. My job is simple."

"Come here to me," she begged, motioning for him to join her on their bed once again.

"Of course," he grinned, "I never turn down the chance for morning lovin'."

He quickly unbuttoned his shirt, tossing it to the side and he moved to sit beside her on the bed, ready for a quick session of morning love, but she squashed all hopes for that when she asked, "What were the orders you were reading from the department yesterday?"

"It's nothing we need to talk about right now," he said before leaning in for a kiss.

"Are you being deployed?" she asked, pulling away.

"Not exactly," he said, leaning in once again.

"What does that mean? 'Not exactly'?" she asked as she sat up, moving away from him.

"I'm being sent on assignment."

"What?!" she yelped.

"Please don't be upset. It's not that long. You knew this might happen, Mel. I can't help it. They need someone with my expertise to be in Houston working on the design of the new jets and I'm not able to say no. It's an assignment. I have to go," he explained.

"For how long?" she asked, taking him in her arms, moving closer.

"Six weeks," he said.

"That's *forever*... Can I come?" she glanced to him as he kissed the top of her head and he answered, "No. I have to stay on base. Willis is being assigned too."

"Lucky for you."

"What's that supposed to mean?" he asked.

"You should've just married Willis," she said standing and walking out of the room and down the stairs.

"Melanie?" He rushed after her. "Melanie, talk to me," he said when he caught up to her where she was staring out the living room windows, watching the cars pass by.

"No," she snapped.

"I'll be home before you know it. It won't be like when I was in training, baby. I'm an officer now. I'll be able to call you, and I will have my cell phone on me in whatever office I'm working in. I'll be thinking about you *all* the time. You can count on that."

She turned to look at him, taking one hand and brushing it against his cheek.

"Promise?"

"I already did. Don't you remember? I said that I would always be here for you. Believe it."

FIFTEEN

"I'm going to call every day. I swear I will," he said, hugging her before walking out the front door to leave for Houston.

"I know. It's just so long," she wrapped her arms around his waist, holding him tightly.

"I'll be back before you know it. I love you."

"I love you."

She closed the door and watched him leave with Willis. Then she walked back in to sit on the couch, gazing out the window, watching the leaves fall from the trees, wishing for the day of his return, when Amber texted.

Hey. I know you're moping around because Jamie left today. But not anymore! Let's get you out of that house! Meet me for lunch!

Happy to have such a spirited friend, she readily agreed and met Amber at the little café near the bridal shop where Amber worked.

"Hi there!" Amber waved, as Melanie walked into the café.

"Hi," Melanie took off her jacket and sat down.

"Tell me. What's been going on? It's always Melanie and James these days and never Mel and Amber anymore! James always wants to hang out with Willis, so naturally Will takes Kay, and poor Amber is left all alone in the singles club of one."

Melanie laughed. "I'm sorry. It's hard for me to deny Jamie anything. I promise we'll do whatever you want while he's gone. Hey! You should come stay with me. I'm nervous to be in that huge house all alone. It could be fun!"

Amber pondered the thought for a moment before agreeing, "Six weeks living off my brother and sister-in-law?

Eating their food, using their utilities, watching their cable? Count me in!"

Melanie laughed once more and thought how having Amber around was going to make Jamie's absence that much more tolerable, but was also going to infuriate James when he found out. She decided she wouldn't tell him until she Facetimed him that night and he heard Amber in the background.

"Amber," Melanie whispered.

"What?" Amber said.

"I know that man." She pointed to the corner of the café where there was a man sitting with his legs crossed, and had his face buried in a newspaper, but he still seemed to be focused on watching her intently.

"You *do*?" Amber turned around, obviously looking at the man.

"Amber!" Melanie reproved.

"What?" Amber asked, uncertain of the nature of Melanie's concern.

"Don't look at him!" Melanie scolded.

Amber shrugged and started looking through the menu for something to eat, while Melanie sent a quick text to James.

Hey. I know you're probably in the air, but when you land, I want you to know two things: 1. I love you and I miss you already. 2. I think I saw that guy who assaulted me in New Haven. I'm pretty sure he was in the café today.

"What'll you girls have today?" the waitress said, walking up, as Melanie slipped her phone away.

"Do you have that amazing chili and cornbread?" Melanie asked.

"Oh honey, we always have that this time of year," she answered

"I want that with a sweet tea."

"Same," Amber said.

"It'll be right out," the waitress said as she took the menus and walked away.

"What's all this fuss about that creepy man in the corner?" Amber asked.

Melanie situated herself in her chair, facing away from him, and she motioned for Amber to lean closer. "That's the man who assaulted me in New Haven."

"What!" Amber screeched.

"Shh! He'll hear you! I sent Jamie a text."

"Right. He didn't text back yet?" she asked.

"No," Melanie replied.

Amber took out her phone and texted her dad to let her know of the situation, and immediately he replied but said that he was headed out for a flight and that they should notify his friend at the department.

Knowing her dad was talking about the weird guy who always brought the sausage links to her mom's holiday parties, she said, "My dad is on duty. Let's just eat and you can wait for Jamie to respond. He's not going to do anything in the middle of the café."

"You're right. Surely, it's got to be a coincidence that he's even here," Melanie said. "He didn't even know my name and it's been over a year and a half since then."

After eating, Amber returned to work, and Melanie went home to call James, hopeful that his plane had landed.

"*Mel?*" he answered. "*Is everything alright, babe? I got your text. Are you sure about that?*"

Just happy to hear his voice, grateful that he was safely on the ground, she locked the door and walked inside, mentioning nothing else of her suspicions.

"Everything's fine. I just wanted to hear your voice. No, I'm not positive it was..."

The first days passed slowly and Melanie missed James terribly, but he did as he said and he called her every day, until one evening when Melanie was nearly ready for bed and he hadn't yet called.

"What do you think is the problem?" she asked Amber as they folded laundry together, waiting for James's call.

"I'm sure he's just working late. Don't worry. He's called you every day since he's been gone," Amber reassured.

"You're right. I'm sure he's just working late."

"You alright tonight?" Willis asked James as they sat down together at the local bar, joining some other officers and airmen for some drinks.

"Yeah, just have something on my mind," he said, sighing.

"Melanie?" Willis asked, knowing entirely that's what it was.

James glanced over, nodding.

"Well, fret no more, my friend! Whiskey sours are coming your way! We've only got two weeks to go here and then your woman will be back in your arms and I can..."

"What? Start messing around with my sister again?" James replied with a smirk.

Willis laughed and said, "Hey now, she's a willing a consenting adult. I can't help it if your sister likes 'em big and dark."

"Shut the hell up. That's my sister, man!" James laughed, giving him a brotherly shove.

183

"Hi gentleman!" a woman approached, interrupting them.

"Do we know you?" James asked the red-haired woman now standing next to them.

"No. But I hope to soon get to know you. My name is Denise. I'm soon being transferred to your base and I hear you want to get into NASA."

"This is true. But what's it to you?" James asked her, then looking to Willis.

"Well, my father is the head of admissions there," she said winking. "Want to buy me a drink?"

"I'm a happily married man to a beautiful woman. But I would like to know more about your father," he said.

"Sorry. Information for serious inquiries only." She blew him a kiss and walked away.

James looked to Willis and downed his whiskey sour.

"How was your day?" Melanie asked when he called her a few hours later.

"It was fine," he said, wanting to tell her that he missed her terribly and wanted to come home.

"I miss you so much. Just come home already," she said, watching him set the phone down, as he angled it to talk and change at the same time, and she admired him while he moved around only half-clothed.

"I want to come home too, babe. Just two more weeks and I'll be there. Willis is aching to get back too."

"Why'd you call so late tonight?" she asked.

"We went out for drinks," he answered, picking up his phone and walking over to lay down on the bed.

"Oh. Who's 'we'?" she asked.

"Willis, of course. Who'd you think I meant?"

She sighed. "No one. I'm just missing you so badly." She looked away from the phone.

"Hey, babe."

"Yeah?"

"Look at me," he said.

Looking back to his Facetime she said, "Just come home to me."

"Two weeks."

"Was there really no one else of any significance at the bar tonight?" she asked.

He thought about telling her about the woman being transferred and how he might have an opportunity to meet the admissions officer, but then he realized Melanie would only be jealous of the idea, and he didn't want her frustrated about nothing. He answered, "No one."

"Okay. I love you."

"I love you," he said.

Two weeks later, James returned, as did Willis, and life was pretty normal, until they were greeted with a new face at his office.

"Hello?" Melanie answered her cell one afternoon as she stood in line at the grocery store, waiting to check out.

"*Hey, babe,*" James replied.

"What's up?" she asked while she loaded her things onto the conveyor belt.

"*Where are you?*" he asked.

"At the store. Why?"

"*I left some documents I need at the house. Can you bring them to me when you're finished?*" he asked.

"Okay. Where are they?"

"That'll be one hundred ninety seven dollars and 52 cents..." the cashier said, as Melanie continued speaking with James.

"*It's a good thing I make nice money, Mel. Yeesh, woman,*" he chuckled. "*What did you buy?*"

"Food. You like to eat," she answered and slid her credit card into the machine.

"Thank you. Have a good day," the cashier said.

"Thanks. You too," Melanie responded to her.

"Okay. I'm done," she said to James as she pushed the cart, walking away. "Now, what is it I'm to do?"

He told her where to find the documents he wanted, and she hurried home to unload the groceries and then headed over to his office, only to be greeted by a surprising sight.

"Good afternoon, Mrs. Hunter," the gate security personnel said her as she drove up. "I'll let Lieutenant know you're here."

When she entered the offices, James wasn't in there, which sparked her curiosity since he would've been expecting her, but she made herself at home nonetheless and sat down at his desk, nosing through all his things. She noticed her picture immediately to her left, which pleased her and she smiled at the sight of the first picture he'd ever taken of her sitting on that bridge.

"Hey, Melanie," Willis said, walking in.

"Hey! What are you up to?" Melanie replied, happy to see him.

"Just the ususal. I like to blow things up. You know that," he said with a grin.

"Where's my man?" she asked, as Willis walked over and sat on the edge of the desk.

"Oh, uh, I think they have him testing specs on a missile..."

"Hey there James!" Denise— the woman they'd been introduced to in Houston— walked in, interrupting.

Melanie's head snapped up at the sound of a woman's voice.

"Oh. You're not the Lieutenant," Denise said.

"Uh oh..." Willis mumbled, letting out a cough.

"No. I'm not. I'm his wife," Melanie replied, staring her down, fiercely.

"I see. He *did* mention you," she said with her arm extended, walking over toward Melanie, "I'm Denise. I just transferred here."

Reluctantly, Melanie shook her hand and said, "Hello. What do you do here?"

"I'm one of the drafters and designers. I work with James on many of the testing modules. He hasn't mentioned me?"

"No. But he doesn't really discuss work at home," Melanie said.

"Well, he seems to enjoy working with me," Denise smiled. But Melanie looked to Willis, who shrugged, shaking his head, disagreeing.

"Is there a party in my office I wasn't informed about?" James asked as he walked in.

"Hi, James," Denise said, looking him up and down.

But he ignored her, walking over to Melanie immediately, planting a kiss on her lips, wrapping his arms around her. "Hey gorgeous. Sorry to keep you waiting. Were you here long?"

"No. Where were you?" she asked, as he ushered everyone out.

"Okay, people. Out of my office... Willis, don't you have something to blow up? Denise, did you need something? Oh, by the way, this is my wife Melanie. Mel, this is Denise. She is one of the new drafters here."

"Yeah. We've just been briefly introduced," she said. "I draw up all the plans, and then James here makes sure I do my job correctly. He's very important!"

Melanie smiled, looking up at him, grasping his fingers in hers, saying, "Yeah. He's a pretty special guy."

Looking to Melanie, Denise said, "Alright then, I'll let you get back to it." And she waked out.

James walked over and sat at the chair behind his desk, motioning for Melanie to join him.

"Glad you're here," he said, "You don't come visit me when I'm working."

"You never invite me. Now I see why," she responded with a quick glance to the door.

"What do you mean?" he asked.

"Nothing. Never mind... I brought those papers you wanted. What are they?" she asked.

"Oh. They're the designs I have to go over on a new jet in the making. It's a beauty. Look..." He held the prints out for her to look at all the lines and figures he had been working on.

"You're such a brainiac," she said, moving herself down from sitting on his desk to his lap, pulling him close to her. "How'd I marry a genius, while I'm just an average girl?"

"You are anything but average, my beauty," he said, taking her chin in his hand to shift her face to look her in the eyes. "But I'm definitely not a genius. The only genius thing I've ever done was marry you." He kissed her.

"Hey man," Willis walked back in, "Kay just called. Wants to know if you two want to have drinks tonight?"

James looked to Melanie questioningly and Melanie turned to Willis giving him a thumbs up.

"Tell her okay, but with one condition," she said.

"Alright. What's that?" he asked.

"She has to bring a date for Amber," Melanie replied, looking back to James, who was shaking his head at Melanie's scheming.

"I have the perfect guy," Willis said, walking away.

"See what you've done," James said, chuckling, planting another kiss on her lips. "Who the hell knows what idiot Will is going to show up with tonight."

"Well, it's better than no one! Poor Amber gets left out of everything these days," she said, kissing his cheek. "I better let you get back to work. I'll see you at home later." She blew him a kiss as she walked to the door.

"Hey," he said.

"Yeah?" she answered and turned in the doorway to look back at him.

"Thanks for marrying me. I love you."

SIXTEEN

Amber had no idea she was being set up on a blind date, so when Willis strolled into the bar that evening with another officer from the base, she scolded Melanie immediately.

"I know what you're up to! It won't work!"

"I don't know what you're talking about," Melanie replied.

"I see that guy with Willis," she said, as the average height, brown haired, medium built man with Willis sat down across from them, and spoke to James.

"James! How's it going? Willis didn't tell me you were as ugly out of uniform as you are in it!" he laughed.

"Lawton, we need to get some liquor in you," James replied.

"Is this your wife? Tell me it isn't. She's far too pretty to be your wife, James," Lawton said.

"I belong to him," Melanie said proudly, leaning in and looking up at James. "I'm his Mrs."

"Well, that's a shame. You're too attractive to be married to this ugly guy," Lawton said.

Melanie blushed deeply and looked to James, saying, "I always thought James was quite the looker."

"It's only because they're so intimidated by my brute masculinity, babe."

"Ha. No. Really it's because your wife is far too attractive to be married to you!"

"Would you stop hitting on my wife?" James said. "I'll bust your ass into next week.

"Someone change the subject," Lawton said before he asked. "What about you, Willis? Who can you claim?"

"Unfortunately, he claims me," Kaylee said, winking at Willis. Everyone at the table laughed, as Willis playfully wrapped his arms around her, sloppily kissing her cheek and Kaylee shoved him away, shouting, "Stop!"

"What about you?" Lawton said to Amber, "Who do you belong to, cutie?"

Amber glared at Melanie for a moment while Melanie gave her a playful wink, and Amber replied, "No one."

"How about I buy you a drink?" he asked.

And James interrupted, "That's my sister."

But Lawton pointed to Willis and said, "Isn't she your sister too? And Willis is like your best friend. They've been banging for like..."

"Woah, man. Fine." James shook his head. "Buy her a drink if you want. But please, no more references to banging my sisters."

Melanie and Willis laughed. Kaylee and Amber rolled their eyes, while Lawton raised his arm, hailing the waitress.

"So, Lawton, what do you do at the base?" Melanie asked, but was interrupted by an annoying voice.

"Fancy seeing you all here!" Denise said, pulling up a chair, sitting on the end of the table on the opposite side of James.

Melanie scooted her chair closer to James, wrapping her arm around his, and intertwined her fingers in his hand.

"Did you invite that woman?" Melanie whispered, as she leaned closely.

"No. I don't know why she's here. Maybe Willis mentioned it. Do you not like her?" he asked.

"She's a bit much, you know, personality wise."

"She is friendly," he said.

"What'll ya'll have tonight, folks?" the waitress asked.

"Just a beer and some wings," Willis said.

"Same for me," Kaylee said.

"That's right, baby. You eat those wings," Willis said to her.

"Knock that off," James said to Willis.

"Consenting," Willis grinned.

"And for you?" the waitress asked Melanie.

"Fries and..." she paused to think for a moment, glancing over to the woman conversing with her husband, "No fries, just a water with lots of lemon, and a chicken salad."

"And for you?" she looked to James. "That burger and the whiskey?"

"Yeah," he said, but then looked to Melanie, noticing her upset. "But also an order of fries," he added.

"Mel? What's wrong?" he asked her.

"Nothing."

"That's a lie. I've never seen you eat a salad in our whole two years married," he said quietly.

"I'm on a diet."

"Whatever. You don't need to be." He shrugged. "I'll take you home later and show how much I think that."

"So, Melanie," Denise said, "How do you spend your time? Do you work?"

Leaning forward to look around James and look at Denise, she replied, "No. James spoils me. I spend my days doing whatever I want. But I would like to go to school to get a degree in something eventually."

"Aren't you bored just sitting at home waiting for your husband all day?" she asked.

"Sometimes, but it's what Jamie wants from me and I would do anything for him."

"You don't want Melanie to have a job, James?" Lawton chimed in.

"That's not it at all. She is welcome to do whatever she wants. It's just that we don't need the money and I figured she'd rather spend her days doing stuff she enjoys. If she wants to get her hair done, so be it. If she wants to go shopping, fine. Visit amber? Go ahead. I make enough money, so why should a job hold her back if she doesn't need to have one? Especially because we want a family someday. My only wish is that my baby is happy," James said, leaning over, kissing Melanie's cheek.

"Sounds like a good enough deal to me, Melanie," Lawton said.

"Me too," Amber said.

"Yeah," Kaylee added, "Where do I get myself a deal like that?" She looked at Willis, who smirked and shrugged, looking away to avoid the question.

"I am spoiled. I won't deny that. The freedom of being able to do what I want every day is nice. Also, I like being there for James when he needs me. There have been times when he's forgotten things or he's needed something to eat and I've been able to take it to him, but if I was working, I wouldn't have been able to do that for him."

"So, what's interesting about you?" Denise asked.

"It's time..." Willis said, standing, walking over to the juke box, turning on a song.

As soon as Melanie heard the song, she smiled and stood, rushing to the middle of the bar to show Denise *exactly* what she was made of... and Shania Twain's song played and she kicked up her feet, clapped her toes and heels on the floor, and twirled around as the words and music played... "Don't be stupid, you know I love you..."

James watched in amazement at his wife's talent and looked to Denise and said, "You were wondering what was interesting about my wife?"

When the song ended and Melanie returned to the table, she looked to Denise and asked, "Do you like to dance?"

But Denise stayed silent, looking to Lawton for conversation.

"Way to shut her the hell up, babe," James said.

"How about some pool while we wait for the food?" Willis suggested.

"Sounds great," James said, grabbing Melanie's hand and jumping up off his chair to race to the back of the bar to the pool tables, pulling her along behind him.

"Jamie," Melanie whispered, wrapping her arm around his waist as he reached for a pool stick.

"What's up?" he answered.

"Why is that woman so interested in me? And why is she so friendly with you?"

"Denise?" he asked as he chalked the end of his stick and kissed the top of her head.

"Yes. Don't you notice?" she asked, and looked back to Denise, who was looking over to them.

"Nope. Haven't noticed at all. But I suppose that could be because I don't care who is interested in me. The only woman I care about is you."

"Hey over there!" Willis hollered to them. "Are we gonna play, or what?"

"Don't be in such a rush to get your ass whooped, Will!" James replied.

"Bring it, lover!" Willis said, motioning for James to come at him.

"Hey!" Kaylee exclaimed, "Aren't I your lover?"

"No. You're confusing the two, my sweets. He's my lover. You're just my girlfriend," Willis said, only to cause aggravation from Kaylee.

"Well, now I know where I rank. If there was a fire and you had to save one of us, I better start praying because I'm going up in smoke!" she said, rolling her eyes.

"Don't be silly," Willis said, "I'd go back in for you."

James and Melanie laughed, but Denise asked, "James, who would you save? Melanie or Willis?"

"Now there's a question!" Willis hollered out. "Your brother of another color or your wife? Who's it gonna be, buddy?"

"Melanie, obviously," James said, giving Melanie a flirtatious wink.

"Damn, man. You're just gonna let me go up in smoke like that? What's a guy got to do to get some love around here?" Willis said.

"You know what that is?" Kaylee said. "That right there, Will, is karma. You let me go up in smoke, so now it's your turn."

Willis laughed, grabbing Kaylee, giving her a soft kiss, before turning to James and saying, "For real, man? You would let me burn?"

"Well, I'm not going to let my wife burn. Honestly, I would figure out a way to save both your asses. Then I would ask you idiots what the hell you're still doing inside a burning building!"

Melanie laughed and said, "You are all ridiculous. I would just get myself out! I'm not waiting for anyone to save me!"

"That's my girl." James winked.

The waitress brought their food over to them at the pool tables, just then, and that's when Melanie realized...

"James," she leaned in, whispering, "Where's Amber?"

He glanced around the area and to the neighboring pool tables but didn't notice her. He shrugged.

"I have no clue. Why?"

"Well, your friend from the base is missing too."

James looked to Melanie, wide-eyed, and asked, "Do you think?"

Melanie shrugged. "Let's hope so!"

The rest of the evening went smoothly and they played pool, ate, and enjoyed their time out with friends, mostly, until

Melanie noticed an alarming figure in the far corner of the room.

"James," she said.

Having already had a few whiskeys, he was not feeling entirely himself. But he turned away from Willis and answered, "What's up?"

"Over there," she said, and pointed to the man sitting in the corner.

Indiscreetly, he turned to look, and even in his half-drunken state, he recognized who it was.

"I'll kill him."

"No, James. Just call the police or something. You've had too many whiskeys. You shouldn't," Melanie said, clutching his arm.

"To hell with that," he said and snatched his arm away. Walking over to the other side of the room, James quickly made a display for the whole bar to see...

"Remember me?" James said to him, sitting down across from him at his table. "See that woman over there? I see you watching her. That's my wife. Stay the hell away from her. I don't know how you found us or what you're doing here in Atlanta. But I have connections, and I'll pull my rank with you. You stay away from my wife. Understand?"

But the scrawny little man wasn't at all intimidated, though James was nearly twice his size, and he leaned forward on the table and said, "Happy to see you again. She's looking as good as ever." Then he licked his lips.

At his words, something inside James snapped, and he dove across the table, snatching the man up by the neck, pounding against the wall behind him, saying "You stay the fuck away from my wife or I swear to everything in life that I'll kill you, you sick son of a bitch!"

"Go ahead and fight me," the man said, egging James on. "That's exactly what I want."

"Jamie," Melanie said, running up. "Just stop."

"Yeah, Jamie," the man provoked. "Be an agreeable husband. Are you always agreeable? Or is she the agreeable one?" He Looked to Melanie and winked. "Hey there, sweetheart. How've you been?"

"Don't even look at her!" James said, giving him a strong right hook, laying him out on the floor.

"James!" Melanie shrieked.

"Great..." Willis sighed. "I better call the commander."

SEVENTEEN

"Willis said the Colonel was coming over this morning," Melanie told James, while he sat in the jail cell and Melanie stood outside.

"Good morning," Denise said, walking up with a man.

"Denise?" Melanie said, looking to the man with her.

"Good morning, James. I'm assuming you are Mrs. Hunter?" he said to Melanie.

"Yes. You are?" she asked.

"My name is Captain Hugh Sharp. I'm here for your husband."

"This is my father, James. The one I told you about in Houston," Denise said.

Nervously, James stood and looked to Melanie, wondering what her reaction would be to Denise's words. But Melanie didn't say anything as they walked out of the jail.

"I have a crew of men looking into the man who is possibly following your wife, Lieutenant," Captain Sharp said as they exited the building. "Also, we received your application. It's been noted," but when he said that, he looked to Denise. Melanie wondered what he meant by that, and she was sure to mention it when they got to the truck.

"You said you didn't meet anyone of significance in Houston."

"I'm sorry. I just knew you would be jealous. I know how..."

"No!" Melanie interrupted, "I'm more upset that you're keeping secrets from me! She likes you James. She'll jump in an instant for an opportunity with you."

"But I don't want her, baby. I only want you," he said.

"That's good. And I want to hear that. But let me see it too."

A few weeks went by and things went pretty much back to normal. A restraining order was put against her attacker from New Haven, so he was no longer allowed within 50 yards of her, which made them feel much more comfortable.

But their relationship started feeling strained when James began spending longer hours at work, going in earlier and coming home after dinner. He used the excuse that he had extra designs to test and that he was unusually busy, and Willis said that he'd tried talking to him, but even Willis couldn't get through to him. Melanie decided to use her best defense...

"Hey, why don't you come back to bed with me? It's awfully chilly this morning. I could use your warmth. It looks like it's going to snow." She pointed to their bedroom window and pulled the blankets over herself.

"I really can't, Mel. I'll be late," James said before he walked over and kissed her forehead. He quickly answered a text and she tried to take a peek as he shoved it away.

"Who was that?" she asked.

"No one," he responded, then he walked out the door.

Sighing heavily, she said to herself, "Honeymoon's over."

A few minutes later Amber texted:

Hey Mel! Let's have lunch!

She texted back:

Okay. But not the bar.

After showering and dressing, she met Amber at the café for lunch.

"Hey girl! It's been like a week since we've had lunch! What have you been doing?" Amber exclaimed as Melanie sat down.

"Just hanging around, doing some shopping... I don't know," she shrugged.

"Hi ladies!" a waitress came up. "What'll it be?"

"I'll have the shredded BBQ chicken sandwich with a sweet tea," Amber said.

"Just the chicken salad for me, please," Melanie said. "With a water and lemon.

"A salad?" Amber asked.

"Can I ask you something?" Melanie asked and started to cry.

"Oh no... Mel. What is it?" Amber wondered.

"You never thought your brother would get married. Why?" Melanie said.

"Are you guys having trouble? What's going on?" Amber sighed.

"Just answer me," Melanie said.

"He was just always so focused on school. He wasn't into relationships with girls. When there was a girl he brought around, she was never around more than once. Why?"

"I think... he's... having an affair," Melanie sobbed.

"Oh god..." Amber gasped. "Why, Mel? What makes you think that? Surely it's not what you think it is."

"For the past several weeks, he's texted me telling me he needs to stay late to work. And when I try to convince him to go in late for 'extracurriculars,' like we used to do..." she paused, crying for a moment.

"It's okay, you can tell me. We'll get it figured out," Amber reassured.

"He just tells me he's going to be late and kisses my forehead."

Amber dropped her head onto the table and thought for a moment to think.

"I don't think this proves he's having an affair," she finally said.

"You don't?" Melanie wiped her eyes.

"No. You're going to that Ball with him tomorrow night, right?" Amber asked, lifting her head.

"Yes."

"Good. Let's eat. Then we'll get you a dress and make you look fantastic. I'll ask Kaylee if I can go with Willis instead of her, and be I'll be your lookout. Okay?"

"Okay..." she whimpered, wiping her tears. "Amber?"

"Yeah, sweetie?"

"Thanks," she sniffled. "You're the best friend ever."

Amber dialed Kaylee. "Kay, we have a situation..."

After they ate, Amber and Melanie picked out a gorgeous dress and shoes to be sure she would stand out at the Air Force Ball. If James was having an affair, he would take one look at Melanie and regret his decision immediately. Not one girl in that hall would come close to looking as fabulous as Melanie in her red, satin, one- shoulder dress, that flowed softly to the floor and hugged her figure just enough to drive him crazy.

"Babe, you about ready?" James yelled up to Melanie from the bottom of the stairs, as she put the finishing touches on her hair in their master bathroom.

"Yes!" she hollered down, not ready to admit that she didn't even have her dress on yet.

"I'm going to wait in the truck. Alright?"

"Whatever!" she yelled back, upset that he wasn't being patient. Sending a quick text to Amber, she shared her frustration:

He's definitely having an affair. He didn't even wait inside for me while I was getting ready! I'm so nervous. I think it might be one of those female officers. *Angry emoji*

Immediately, Amber replied:

Don't make any assumptions yet. You know Jamie. He can just be a butthead sometimes. Mel, he loves you. We both know that. Let's just see how things go. *Kiss emoji*

Melanie put on her stunning red dress, which fell just softly to the floor and over her silver shoes. After adding a pair of diamond, dangle earrings and the heart necklace from James, she grabbed her purse and rushed down the stairs to see him still waiting at the door.

"You look... amazing." He smiled as he looked to her walking his way.

"Thanks. You always look great in your dress blues," she replied, taking his arm, walking together to the truck.

"Let me help you up," he said, hoisting her into the truck, while also taking a nice feel of her in the thin material of her dress.

"Jamie!" she yelled out playfully. "What are you doing?"

"Just taking a feel, enjoying what's mine," he said as he closed the truck door and walked around the front, winking at her.

She shook her head, smiling admiringly at him, reconsidering that maybe he wasn't having an affair, thinking it was possible she was overreacting.

"I thought you said you were going to wait in the truck?" she asked.

"I changed my mind. I've been known to do that sometimes."

A small gasp escaped from her mouth at his words, thinking he was also referring to his feelings about her. Turning to look out the window, allowing a few tears to roll down her cheeks, she swallowed her feelings and also her fear, watching the cars pass by on the street, wondering what she'd done to lose his love and interest so quickly.

"Amber!" Melanie hollered as she and James walked into the large ballroom and James immediately noticed Amber with Willis.

"Amber? What's she doing here? Where's Kaylee?" James questioned.

"Oh... Uh..." Melanie mumbled, trying to come up with a logical reason to explain Amber's presence, *other* than that they were going to spy on all his activities that evening to be sure that he wasn't getting too intimate with any females at the base.

"Melanie? Why is Amber here?" he asked again.

"Kaylee didn't want to come and Willis was afraid to look like a *loser*," Amber said, walking up from behind James. "C'mon, Mel. Let's go get a drink and we'll let James mingle." She linked arms with Melanie whispering, "We need to watch what he's doing," and they walked away.

"Okay," Melanie whispered in reply, turning her head just slightly to watch James's actions, but quickly looking ahead when she saw his eyes fixed upon her, as he watched her walk to the refreshments with Amber, admiring her beautiful figure outlined by her sexy red dress, thinking he'd won the wife jackpot. Though, his thoughts were soon interrupted by Willis.

"Hey, man!"

"Hey," James responded, still watching Melanie.

"What's up? Whatcha thinking?" Willis asked.

"You don't want to know what I'm *actually* thinking," he smiled slightly and pointed at Melanie munching on a few carrots.

Willis nodded, chuckling slightly at his friend's infatuation over his wife and said, "Yes, keep those thoughts to yourself. What else is going on?"

"Something's up with her. She's either *scheming,* or something's bothering her. I can tell that she isn't herself tonight."

"Maybe it's a woman thing." Willis shrugged.

"Maybe. She *can* be moody."

"All women are moody. I'm dating the *queen* of the moody. She wouldn't even come with me tonight. I had to bring princess high horse herself," Willis said, pointing to Amber.

"Ha. Oh, Amber... she only feeds into Melanie's drama."

"Want a drink?" Willis asked.

"Yeah," James replied, as they headed toward the bar.

"Melanie?" a woman approached as she and Amber perused the appetizers.

"Yes?"

"Hi. It's Denise. Do you remember me?"

"Of course," Melanie said.

"How is everything going?" she asked.

"How do you mean?" Melanie said.

"Oh, I just wondered if everything has been okay, you know, with James since that night he got taken in. Thank goodness I was there to help!" she said.

"Yep. Thankful for you," Melanie said sarcastically, looking to Amber.

"Where is he?" she asked, looking around for James.

"Oh, he's with Willis somewhere," Melanie waved her finger in the air, brushing off the comment, noticing that Denise was soon walking away and looking for James. But Melanie resumed speaking with Amber. "How odd she is."

"Mel, I think you should be cautious of that woman," Amber said, pointing to Denise who was hurrying over to James at the bar.

"You think she's the one?" Melanie asked, looking over to Denise, and watching her walk up to James, wrapping her arms around him, embracing him and kissing his cheek. "Oh my!" Melanie exclaimed, gagging on the carrot stick in her mouth.

"Yep. Told you. She's got the hots for your man," Amber sassed.

"I figured as much. But what about Jamie?" Melanie watched as James gently returned the hug. "No..." Melanie's gasped, and her glass dropped from her hand, shattering on the floor, causing a scene as everyone nearby looked over to see what the commotion was. Fortunately, James was too far away to notice what had happened.

"Here, Ma'am. Let me get that for you," a waiter said, and hurried over to clean up the broken glass.

"Thank you," Melanie said as she backed away, choking back her tears.

"Mel, honestly though, maybe it's nothing. It was only a hug," Amber said, taking Melanie's arm as she tried reassuring.

"She has red hair..." Melanie whispered, drowning out Amber's coaching. "I didn't really notice before now, but look..." she said, pointing to Denise and her shoulder length cropped red hair.

"Melanie?" Amber said, rubbing up her arm, knowing that her friend was going into some sort of panic mode. "Okay, I know this shock and panic look from you." Amber watched tears drip from Melanie's eyes, while she also watched the friendly conversation happen between James and the pretty redhead across the room, so she said, "No more of this. I'm getting Willis. You stay right there." Then she walked away.

But Melanie didn't listen. She turned and went for the back-exit doors to grab her checked purse and call a cab.

"My purse please," she handed her ticket to the doorman and walked out, only to be met in the parking lot by a familiar voice.

"You think you can outsmart me with your rules and laws? You think your husband can use his rank in society to keep me away? Do you think that's what it's going to take? When I see something I want, I take it. Your husband has made a fool of me, now he's going to pay for it."

"Amber, where's Melanie?" James asked when Amber walked back with Willis several minutes later.

"I'm not sure. I left her right here," she pointed to the spot where they'd been standing next to the refreshment table.

"Why did you leave her at all?" James questioned.

"Why were *you* over *there* with little missy kissy face?" Amber sassed.

"What?" he replied, unknowing of what she was talking about.

"You know, maybe your *wife* was upset about seeing *you* with that woman who was a little too hands on, James."

"You mean Denise? No. Melanie knows better than that. Denise is just a friendly woman. Tell me Melanie doesn't think... she doesn't believe that I... does she?! Amber?!" he asked, surprised at what was playing out in front of him.

"James, you're married now. You can't be friendly with women the way you once were, even if *they* want to be friendly with *you*. Despite your intentions being honorable, your wife doesn't want to see that."

"Shit. I never thought. Does she think?" James panicked.

"Yeah, James. She does," Amber sassed.

He let out a frustrated sigh, walking a few angry circles where he was standing, running his hands over his face. "Did she go home?"

"Beats me. Go ask the doorman if she checked out her things, or maybe call her cell. Better yet, I'll call her. She'll answer *me*."

James hurried over the door to check for her things. "Did the woman with the other end of this ticket already take her things?"

"Yes, sir," he replied.

"About how long ago?"

"Ten minutes or so. She left just outside those doors right there, I believe." The doorman pointed to the side exits where Melanie left towards the truck.

"Thank you," James said and hurried outside, thinking that it was possible she was waiting at the truck and blowing off steam. But when he approached the scene, his breath escaped him and he dropped to his knees when he saw Melanie's purse opened and its contents spilled out on the ground next to the passenger side, along with a folded-up piece of paper, which read: "I won't be made a fool of again. I won't abide by your laws. Who's the bitch now?"

"James?" Willis hurried up beside him, Amber following behind, as James just kneeled, staring at the note.

"He took her," James said

"Who took her?" Willis asked, grabbing at the note, noticing her mace had been sprayed and was on the ground with everything else.

After reading it, he looked down to James, who only said, "She's my wife. Tell me she's okay. Willis, tell me she's going to be okay. I..." He paused, shaking his head, breathing heavily, punching his fists into the side of his truck.

Willis grabbed his shoulders steadily in his hands and said, "Just go home, James. We got this man. She's gonna be fine."

"She's my whole world," James said, and walked around to his side, as he hopped in, and angrily screamed out, before he slammed his door closed. He collapsed his head onto the steering wheel and finally gave into his frustrations, allowing himself to cry.

"I need to report a missing person," Willis said to the 911 operator. Then he dialed the base to alert the commanding officer of the situation.

EIGHTEEN

"How many hours has it been, Will?" James asked as he poured himself another shot of whiskey and they waited for the command unit to arrive.

"Only four, buddy. She's only been gone four hours. They're doing their best, man. Just be patient."

James downed his whiskey and turned on the news...

"We are on the search tonight for the wife of a local Air Force officer who went missing earlier this evening. There is evidence to believe that there were some previous encounters with the man in suspect..."

"James, don't watch it," Amber said.

"What the hell else do I have to do?!" he yelled. "You want me to get drunk? I'll get drunk!" He lifted the bottle of whiskey and took a few drinks. "Tell me what I'm supposed to do!"

"Nothing, James. Do nothing," Willis said.

Many shots of whiskey later, and after he'd slept it off, the Colonel arrived with a crew of men to get to work.

"Lieutenant, we want you to know that we are considering this a matter of national concern and even the General has been notified of her disappearance. We are doing everything we can to ensure that she returns home safely."

"Thank you, Colonel," James responded as he watched the command unit set up their supplies in his living room.

"I'm here for you too, buddy," Willis said, resting his hand on James's shoulder. "Whatever you need, consider it done."

"Me too. You know I'm not going anywhere," Amber added, hugging him.

"The wife of an Air Force officer, who works as one of our honored and trusted engineers here at the Warner Robbins

base, has disappeared tonight and authorities believe that the kidnapping might have been provoked by a previous encounter with the attacker..." the newswoman said as someone turned channels on the living room TV.

"It's my fault she disappeared, isn't it?" James asked Amber and Willis, as he stood to get a whiskey.

"Would someone turn that shit off!" Willis yelled as he followed James into the kitchen. "Nah, man. Don't pay attention to that garbage," Willis said, "You know how reporters like blowing everything above what..."

"I'm not just talking about that!" James interrupted, "I'm talking about all of it... about how much of a fucking screw up I am! If I wouldn't have let Denise hug me, then Melanie wouldn't have left, and then she wouldn't..."

"James, stop being so hard on yourself. It's not helping. We're going to find her," Amber encouraged. "Look around you." She motioned to all of the military men, police officers, and FBI agents standing around his house. "The government is pissed. They consider this a threat against them. You are one of them, so *she* is one of them. They're going to nail this son of a bitch."

"I can't lose her, Amber... She saved me," he said, downing his whiskey.

"I know. Give them time. It's only been several hours. You're going to get her back. Stay strong for her."

"Lieutenant..." called one of the agents from the living room. "Could you give us a minute? We would like to go over some details with you again to possibly pin down a location."

"See James? They're already hopeful on a location. Go..." Amber nudged him along.

But Melanie's hope wasn't as strong, as she was being held down to a dirty, metal-framed bed, all four limbs stretched out and tied tightly to each bed post.

"Are you feeling hopeless?" he asked, running his finger along her jawline as she cried.

"No. I know my husband will come. He loves me."

"Is that so? Then why were you leaving that party without him? Why were you walking around New Haven without him? If he loves you *so much* then why do you always seem to be without him?" he mocked.

"I..." she stuttered.

"My theory is this..." He grabbed her face in his hands and climbed on top of her, as she started thrashing her body to protest. "I conclude that he only wants you for the same reasons I do. But *you* want *him* for so much more."

"No!" she spit at his face. "He loves me!"

"Is *that* what it takes to get from you what *he* gets? Telling you 'I love you'?"

"Get off of me!" she screamed, fighting back as best she could, as he tore her dress from her.

"You're right. I'm going to wait. If you're sure he's going to come, let's make him watch. That's the sweetest revenge," her attacker laughed.

"Don't you dare hurt him!" Melanie screamed.

He pulled out a gun, twirling it around on his finger, singing, "Around and around it goes... where it will stop, nobody knows..."

"No!!" Melanie screamed.

FOUR HOURS LATER

After locating her within one mile of their house, the search dogs used her undergarments and other soiled items of clothing to track down a two-block radius and finally pinpointed the house she was being kept inside.

"Lieutenant, she's going to be in a terrified, probably confused, maybe even abused state. Let our teams go in first." Agent Kent said.

"I understand what she'll be like, but I need to see her first. I want her to see me. Please, I'm ready. I was trained for this."

"But not for your own wife, Lieutenant," he tried convincing.

"Please, let me," James asked.

"Just let us enter first to clear the room. We don't know if it's just him in there with her. The scanner has located two bodies in the basement and we believe it to only be them. These types of abusers are smart. He was intelligent enough to locate you down here in Atlanta with only her broken cell phone. Most of them are mentally unhinged and are dealing with serious issues. We have no idea what we are walking into. There's a reason he chased your wife down. Let us investigate what we have going on, with you following in after. Even though you're not a civilian, we still can't risk you getting hurt. Especially for her sake and what she's been through." Agent Kent motioned for the squat to clear the building and then followed in, with James closely behind.

"You hear that?" the attacker whispered to Melanie, "Your husband is here. I can hear them coming in upstairs. Better get the supplies ready."

He walked over to load his pistol, while Melanie let out a shrill of fear through her taped-up mouth as she watched.

"I hear her..." the agent with the listening sonar said as he heard Melanie's muffled cries for help.

James grabbed the sonar, listening carefully and said, "That's her! That's Melanie!" and horror and fear struck every nerve and bone in his body while he listened to the absolute terror in her voice as she cried out.

"Hurry!" he said forcefully but quietly, ushering them along. "We need to get to her."

"She's alive and is yelling for help. We will call that good news, Lieutenant."

As they approached the basement, James immediately saw Melanie on the bed and wanted to rush over to her, as she'd been stripped nearly naked and she was still lying, stretched with all four limbs to each post.

"Where is this son of a bitch? I'm going to kill him," James said as they walked into the basement.

"James!" she screamed the loudest she could through her still taped-up mouth.

"I'm right here," the attacker said as he sauntered his short, skinny body around the corner from behind the stairs and into view, pointing the pistol towards Melanie. "You know, *Lieutenant*, when I brought your wife down here, I wondered... What would be my biggest revenge against you for making a fool of me? I thought about raping your wife. But I didn't. Because then you could just take her home and erase that and have your way with her yourself. I thought about bringing you here and making you watch." He pointed the gun at James, and Melanie shrieked, and Agent Kent said, "Watch yourself, that's a decorated military man you're pointing that gun at. You're going away for two lifetimes or even death row if you pull that trigger."

"Nah, I wouldn't dare dream of killing *him*, it defeats the purpose of my revenge. You see, I need to seek *revenge* on him. How can I get back at *him*, is what I says to myself. So..." He turned to face Melanie and immediately James knew.

"No!!!" James yelled just as he pulled fire, and James jumped into the range of the bullet.

Melanie screeched as she watched James drop onto the floor.

"Hello, we have an officer down. I repeat, we have an officer down," Agent Kent said as he dialed 911 and a shot went out and into Melanie's attacker, taking him down.

"You get her untied, while I see to the Lieutenant. He hasn't much time," Kent ordered, and tried to stop the profuse bleeding coming from James's left shoulder.

"James?!" Melanie screamed. "Is he okay?" she yelled as they took the tape off her mouth, untied her, and covered her with an FBI jacket.

"They're taking him to the hospital at the base. We will take you there too, for a checkup."

"NO! I'm fine. I just want to see him! Let me see him!" she continued yelling, wondering if he was okay or if he was even alive.

"Ma'am, you've..."

"Forget about me! Let me see my husband!" she insisted. "Is he okay?" she asked, but no one answered her.

Once she was untied, she was handed a t-shirt and some sweatpants to wear and an FBI jacket to put on, and immediately she rushed over to James, who was still lying on the floor, bleeding profusely.

"James!" she screeched when she saw his unconscious body. "Where is the ambulance?"

"They're on the way ma'am," Agent Kent said to her, as he instructed the others to cover up the attacker's dead body. "Come with me, Mrs. Hunter."

"No," she refused. "I'm staying right here until the ambulance comes." She cradled James's head in her hands and began to cry.

"The ambulance is here. They're coming down now," he pointed to the stairs.

Watching them load James's nearly lifeless body onto the gurney and carry him away was practically a blur in her mind and it hardly felt real, and she sat in his pool of blood, only staring, her heart pounding in her chest, until Agent Kent reached down and helped her stand, steadying her to the van to take her to the hospital.

Even though they had taken down her attacker, the agents secured the building before they allowed her entrance, which gave the squad several minutes to get James situated before Melanie arrived.

"James Hunter, please," she said to the triage desk, "I'm his wife."

"ER room three. He's currently in surgery, though Ma'am. I can let the ER doctor know you're here."

"Surgery? Thank you." She sighed and walked to the empty ER room, escorted by Agent Kent, who waited outside the door.

"Mrs. Hunter?" the doctor said at her arrival.

"Yes? Hello," she greeted him.

"Your husband's surgery should take just a little longer. Immediately upon his arrival, we knew that he'd need the bullet removed and that we would need to repair the damage to his shoulder. But he will be okay. He is lucky, however; it missed the brachial artery by mere centimeters."

"But he's going to be okay? Can he go home today?" she asked.

"He's going to be fine. But he needs to spend the night and can go home tomorrow."

Breathing a sigh of relief, she replied, "Thank you."

She sat down in the guest chair and laid her head on the window sill to get some rest, thankful that she wasn't going to lose him, and she thought over the last days' events and how she regretted ever walking out on the Ball, but still wondered about Denise and her concerns about James spending more time at work. After sleeping thirty minutes or so, and allowing some worries to interrupt her thoughts, the nurse walked in.

"Mrs. Hunter, come with me. James is in recovery now."

At hearing those words, she pushed all terrible thoughts out of her mind and only focused on seeing his face. She would let him explain his actions himself.

"He's right in here, Ma'am," the nurse said as they approached the recovery room.

"Jamie?" Melanie said, approaching his bedside.

"Mel?" he said.

"Oh my god. I can't believe you took a bullet for me," she started crying and grabbed his face kissing him.

"Easy, Mel. I'm hurting, babe," he groaned and pointed to his arm wrapped up and braced to his chest in order to keep his shoulder from moving. "Of course I took a bullet for you. I would do anything for you, including die for you. Don't you know that?"

"I don't deserve you," she replied, and wiped her tears.

"Hey, why are you crying?"

"I feel guilty," she admitted, saddened by her assumptions about Denise.

"Why? What's going on?"

"This is all my fault. I left the Ball because I thought you were having an affair with that woman, Denise," she sniffled.

"I know." He nodded.

"You do?" she asked.

"Yep. Amber told me. I don't care. I mean, I do. But, what I mean is I'm not angry at you. I guess what I'm trying to say is that I'm going to be a better husband. I'm sorry I'm failing you."

"Oh, Jamie. You're not failing me. I just thought... She has red hair and..."

"Ah. That's what it is? Hey. Promise me something?" he asked.

"Anything. It's the least I can do after you take a bullet for me."

"Stop assuming that I like women because they have red hair. Okay? You are my wife. I married *you*. I only want *you*. I don't want anyone else. Be assured of that. Promise me?"

"Okay. I promise."

"Melanie. I've never taken a bullet for anyone else. That's got to mean something. This really hurts." He pointed with his good hand to his injured shoulder.

"You wouldn't take one for Willis?" she asked.

"No way! That idiot can take it like a man."

She leaned in, kissing him, "I love you, James Tyler. I'm sorry I doubted you. I won't do it again."

"Yes, you will." He teased, brushing the hair away from her forehead.

"Okay, maybe I will."

"But next time, just don't make me take a bullet for it, okay?"

"Deal."

NINETEEN

James woke and did his usual routine of showering and grabbing a quick bowl of cereal. But before he left for the base, he stopped back by the bedroom and saw that Melanie had moved out from under the blankets, giving him a pleasing eyeful.

"Mel." He walked in, waking her, kissing along her neckline and descending down her exposed back, brushing his fingers along her spine.

"Mmm..." she moaned from the teasing he was doing to her, and she rolled over onto her back to see him.

"Good morning, beauty," he kissed her. "I was ready to leave until I walked in here and saw you looking all tempting and sorts." He climbed on top of her, straddling her waist, moving her hair to kiss her neckline.

"Well... as long as you're here..." She started unbuttoning his shirt, exposing his chest.

He leaned in, kissing her some more, while she moved her hands to work on his belt buckle.

"I really have to go," he mumbled as their kissing turned heated and he laid down next to her, pulling her on top of him.

"Then I guess you shouldn't have come in here getting all frisky and naughty, now should you have?" She grabbed his face in her hands and took control, kissing around his ear, then down his neck, impatiently waiting for him to remove his uniform shirt and under shirt.

"You're wearing your short-sleeved blues today. That's unlike you," she said as she watched him toss his shirt to the floor.

He smiled at her and she positioned herself to yank his uniform pants off.

"It's going to be like 95 degrees out there today... scorching," he explained.

She moved back up to his face and he moved over on top of her ready to resume, but she spoke before he could continue with his urges.

"But you're an engineer. Aren't you at a computer all day?"

"Mostly, but I have to work in the yard too, Mel. There's a new jet they're testing and I have to be in the hangar some today while they test some of the specs on it, *especially* because I'm an engineer. You forget that my work includes making sure that everything is running smoothly. I'm very useful to them."

"Well, you're very useful to me too, you know." She kissed his cheek and rubbed up his back and he continued with his desires.

"Melanie, how do you do it?" He sighed, stretching out next to her.

"What?" she asked, running her fingers up and down his chest, teasing his chest hair, leaning in to nibble his ear.

"How do you make me so satisfied yet drive me so insane at the same time?" He moved in to tickle her, causing some giggles and squeals to erupt from her.

"I miss you when you're gone, you know. It's not the same when you're not here," she said as she watched him stand to get dressed.

He smiled at her and said, "I miss you too. You're much better company than the guys at the base." He kissed her forehead.

"I have something for you," she said, leaning over to her nightstand drawer, pulling a letter out.

"What's this?" he looked at it as he finished buttoning his shirt.

"It came for you yesterday," she beamed.

He looked to her, wide-eyed and excited, anticipating the response inside.

August 23, 2018

To: LT. JAMES HUNTER

From: THE DEPT OF THE NATIONAL AEURONAUTICS AND SPACE ADMINISTRATION ADMISSIONS OFFICE

Dear Lieutenant James Hunter,

We are pleased to inform you...

"Melanie!" he exclaimed. "Pack your bags, baby! We are headed for the moon!"

She giggled excitedly as he jumped over on top of her, throwing his arms around her, hugging her tightly.

"Are you happy?" he asked.

She nodded enthusiastically.

"I knew they'd accept you. You're so smart. They'd be so stupid not to!" She kissed him repeatedly as he lifted her onto his lap.

"It's going to be a big change for us, though. We'll have to move away from our family and friends."

"Jamie," she pulled away and said, " *You* are my family now. I love you more than you know. You've changed my whole world these past five years. You're my everything."

"You know it's the same for me too, baby. I told you the day I met you that I was falling in love with you, and every time

I kiss you, I fall harder. Mel, let's spend every day of our lives just like this."

"How's that?" she asked.

"Ridiculously happy," he answered.

He started undressing once again, and they disappeared under the sheets once more.

"You're late today," Willis smirked as James walked into the office at 10:00 instead of 9:00.

"Don't spread your hate to me because Kaylee's a prude," James teased.

"Whatever, man. Just hurry your ass up because they called for you to be out in the hangar like 35 minutes ago. I think Major Jeffries wants you to take a look at that new F-35 fighter we have before they make a test flight."

"I figured so. I better go before someone breaks something I'm going to have to stay late fixing."

He walked out to the hangar to see everyone standing around the new beauty of a jet that he couldn't wait to test.

"Good morning, Major," James said to the older, broad shouldered officer as he approached the men surrounding the plane.

"Hi, Lieutenant. We are having some issues with the thrust mechanisms and we need your expertise. You *are* the one who helped in the design of this beauty, after all."

"Sure thing. Why don't I take her out for a morning test run and see what I can figure out?" James suggested.

"I knew you'd want to give her a go," the major said. "But be careful. I'm not sure where the malfunction is coming from."

"Don't worry. I'll be okay."

James quickly suited up and the airmen gave him the specialized helmet.

After checking on some of the switches, and being certain that everything was ready for his takeoff, he hopped into the cockpit and fired her up, driving the powerful jet out to the runway.

"I think that I would much prefer to live in Texas than Louisiana," Melanie said as she sat in a café having brunch with Janice and Amber.

"Well, wherever you are, I hope you try for a baby again soon," Janice said. I don't expect my other children to produce any grandchildren before I'm too old to enjoy them."

"Don't worry. Jamie desperately wants a son. We will. I'm just nervous about losing another," Melanie said.

"I know, sweetie, but..." Janice's words were interrupted by Melanie's cell.

"Hello?" she answered.

"Mel? It's Willis. There's been an accident."

She rushed into the ER room as quickly as her legs would carry her to see her beloved lying there scorched, burned, and barely holding on for his life. Unable to conceal the despair and grief that expended her mind and spirit right then, she dropped to her knees, covering her heart with one hand and her mouth with the other, letting an anguished gasp escape from her mouth at the sight.

"James!" she cried as she listened to his heart beating on the monitor to show her that there was some hope left because from the look of his burned body, she felt there could hardly be any.

"Melanie," he struggled to say as he moved his arms to reach out to her.

"Jamie?" She hurried to his side and he opened his eyes to look at her.

"You're here. I missed you. I hurt so much. Take away the pain," he muttered, grasping her fingers painfully in his.

"Oh. I don't know how." She looked at his charred face and dropped tears, wishing she could help him. "Willis told me what happened," she cried. "That you were testing a new jet and the engine exploded as you were landing, but that you escaped just before the whole jet burst into flames."

He nodded. "I'm sorry. I thought it was safe enough, Mel. I helped designed that jet and I knew its specs."

"Shh. It's okay. Don't apologize. Did you have fun? Was that jet a good one?" she asked, looking at the sadness in his eyes.

"It was a good one. But I... I'm sorry."

As he laid there watching tears roll down her cheeks, he regretted jumping into that cockpit that morning, and he was wishing he'd thought less of himself and more of the one thing in the world that meant more to him than anything else—her.

"Tell me you're going to be okay. I need you to be okay. We were going to the moon."

"I think..." He stopped and tried to breathe, sounding very much like he was gasping for air. "I think you're going to reach for the stars alone, my love." He closed his eyes once more but held firmly onto her fingers.

"Jamie? James?!" She panicked and called for a nurse. "Is there a nurse or a doctor?! Someone? Is someone out there?! I need help in here! Please!!"

The nurse walked in. "Is something the matter?" she asked.

"He isn't responding to me. Why isn't he talking to me?" she asked, terrified that she was losing him, fearing for his life.

"He has experienced extreme trauma and the doctors have him on a strong pain management regimen. It will be normal for him to feel sleepy. Unless his monitors start beeping, there is no cause for concern. The doctors will be in to talk with you soon. You should rest too. He has a long recovery ahead of him."

Melanie sighed deeply and sat in the chair next to his bed, laying her head directly on his side, kissing his bandage wrapped fingers that were still clinging to hers.

"Jamie, please get better. I don't how to live without you," she said a little while later, after closing her eyes for a nap.

"I'm trying," he whispered.

Sitting up quickly, she exclaimed, "You're awake!"

"I've been for a while, but you were so beautiful there sleeping that I didn't want to wake you. I love you." He carefully lifted his hand and laid it on top of hers where she had it rested on the bed. "I'm worried, Mel."

"No. Don't say that. It's going to be fine. You're going to be fine because you have to be. I need you to get better and come home with me. Okay?"

He didn't nod but just said, "I love you, always."

"Jamie, don't give up on me. You're not giving up on me. Promise me."

He closed his eyes once more.

"James. Jamie? James?!"

Her breath quickened as she let a few tears fall before she walked out to find the doctors, feeling herself falling into a state of distress.

"Hello. I'm Mrs. Hunter. My husband is James Hunter." She pointed behind herself to his room.

"Right. He's the Lieutenant they brought in this morning. What can I do for you?"

"I need you to be honest with me. Tell me what his recovery looks like. Please." She wiped her tears, trying to compose herself.

"Alright. Well, he is severely burned on most of his body, which means he is at a high risk for infection. The upper part of his lung was injured and he is having a difficult time breathing, but we scheduled him for surgery first thing tomorrow to repair the damage to his lung. I'd say his greatest hurdle will be to overcome the risk for infection. Once we clear that, and his burns heal, he can go home, but he'll need some skin graphing."

"How soon do you think he'll be home?" she asked, her heart feeling lighter already.

"Two weeks?"

She smiled and walked back into his room, feeling more hopeful that her husband might be okay after all.

The first days passed slowly, as James seemed to sleep a lot from the pain medications, and it was hard for her to watch them change his bandages every few hours, feeling so bad for the pain he was enduring.

"You might want to go to the hall as we do this, Ma'am," the nurse said.

"Why?" Melanie asked as they prepared to change his bandages.

"Because it's going to be bloody, and it will be painful for him. It might be hard for you to watch."

"I'd like to stay, if that's alright. I care for him," Melanie replied, concerned over the care that he was receiving.

The nurse nodded and began with his arms and chest.

"Agh!" he cried out as she pulled off the old, blood crusted, puss covered, gauze and cloths, then cleaning and wiping it with medications.

"Just hang on there, James," the nurse coached him as he winced and cried out in pain again.

"Agh! I can't! Just stop!" he yelled.

Melanie turned away, tears flowing, unable to watch his pain. Never having been an overly religious girl before in her life, she wasn't sure if there was a right or wrong way to pray. She'd only ever gone to church with her grandparents as a child. But she decided if there was ever a time in her life to try, now might be it.

"God, if you're there, and you can hear me, please don't take him. Make him better. We've been through so much together. I don't why I was given this man or why he was brought into my life, but I need him."

Her words were interrupted by James's shrieks of agony as they continued working on him.

Melanie's cries and pleas continued, "Please. He is so good to so many people. He doesn't deserve this. He has loved me through so much."

"Ma'am?" the nurse tapped her on the shoulder.

Melanie spun around.

"We're finished. He wants to see you."

"Thank you," Melanie wiped her eyes and returned to his bedside.

"Hey. Why are you crying?" he asked, as she sat down beside him once again.

"Jamie, if you don't get better, what am I going to do?"

He took her hand and softly kissed her knuckles, then he said, "You? You're going to accomplish everything that you would've done with your life had you never met me, with one exception."

"What's that?" she cried.

"You're going to take me with you."

"How?" she sobbed.

"Because now you know how to reach for the stars. Mel, you're the greatest thing that's ever happened to me. You made my life complete. You gave me love. But you? I taught you how to trust yourself. You needed that boost, babe. I love you. Reach for the stars."

"Just stay with me," she laid her head next to him and sobbed.

"Melanie," he whispered, "Lay with me. Right here," he patted on his chest, and she moved her whole body onto the bed to lay with him. He stroked her hair, pulling her in closely, despite the pain it was causing to have her against his skin. "I'm sorry I didn't do right by you." He leaned down to kiss her forehead as she cried.

"No. Don't you ever think that. I've never believed for even one second of my life with you that you were a mistake. I won't know what to do with myself if you leave me," she sobbed, clutching ahold of his hospital gown. "Tell me it's all going to be okay. Just lie to me."

"In the end, it will be, Mel. If it's not okay, it isn't the end, not yet. You're going to have a beautiful life. I promise you."

But after receiving his lung repair and being able to breathe easier, things seemed to be looking up. His skin was healing and the antibiotics were keeping away the risk of any infections.

"Melanie," he said one morning as she stared out the hospital window.

"Good morning," she walked over and kissed his now healing lips.

"When was the last time you ate or had anything to drink. When was the last time you slept?"

She shrugged.

"Please take care of yourself. Do it for me. Look at me. I'm getting better. Go to the cafeteria and eat something. Go home and shower. I'll be here when you get back. I love you."

She sighed, not wanting to do what he said, but obeyed nonetheless.

When she returned, she saw that he was sleeping peacefully, so she walked over, kissed him, also waking him.

"Jamie, I'm back."

He smiled and opened his eyes, inhaling deeply, but as he did, he started coughing heavily.

"Mel, get the doctor. I can't breathe." He started coughing heavier, breathing deeper, gasping for air. Then he started spitting up blood all over himself, as Melanie screamed for help.

"Someone, get in here!!" She shouted into the hallway but looked to James in distress, watching him hold his chest and struggle to breath, coughing blood all over. "Help!!" she cried.

The doctor and nurses came running in, pushing her out, sending her into a fret.

"God, I don't even know if there is a god, but if you are there," she prayed. "I love this man and I need him. Please don't take him from me. I'll do anything." She dropped to her knees, pleading.

Many minutes later, the doctor walked out, closing the curtain and door behind him.

"Mrs. Hunter."

"James?! No! No!!!" she begged as she sobbed. "It can't be! Go back in there and fix this! Do *something*! Please!!! You *have* to fix this!!" she cried as she fell forward and the doctor caught her in his arms.

"We are so sorry, Ma'am. His lung threw a clot and..."

"No!" She dropped down, crying violently, just as Janice walked up, thinking she was bringing Melanie something to eat.

"What is it?" Janice asked.

The nurse took over comforting Melanie's sobs, while the doctor knew he was going to have a despondent mother on his hands.

"Oh!" Janice cried out as she quickly rushed to the closed doors. "My son!" she cried. "Oh, my Jamie!" She banged on the doors.

Amber and Kaylee approached the scene along with Willis, and immediately they knew.

"Oh god." Amber teared up as she saw Melanie crouched down on the floor, hands pulling at her hair, cries screaming out, and she walked over to her mother as she saw the closed door and pulled it open. "Go ahead Melanie and Mom. Say goodbye."

Melanie rushed in to his bed, pulling his lifeless body up to her as she cradled him in her arms, lying down on the bed next to him.

"Jamie..." she wept. "Come back to me... tell me you love me again. Please..." She cried as she held his body against hers.

Janice walked around to the other side of the bed, stroking his hair with her fingers as she cried and Melanie hugged him.

Amber sat down in the chair next to his bed and reality struck her, while she watched heartbreak consume Melanie and her mother, and she just sat, letting tears flow from her eyes. But Kaylee couldn't handle it, so she grabbed Willis and walked out of the room to deal with her pain in the hallway.

"Janice?" Melanie wept.

"Yes, sweetie?"

"What am I going to do?"

"You're holding him in your arms. Ask yourself what he would say to you."

"Reach for the stars..." she imagined him saying just like he used to.

TWENTY

The preacher looked to her mother, motioning for her to soothe the crying, and he began his service. "We are here to remember the life of and military service of Lieutenant James Tyler Hunter. Let us pray."

At the beginning of his words, Melanie leaned forward resting her face against the casket, trying to get one last feel of Jamie's presence, kissing the smooth surface before she said, "I love you. Don't leave me. We didn't have enough time. Please stay with me." Then she stood and backed away from the casket with her hand placed on her chest over her heart, breathing heavily.

"I can't... I can't do this," she said as she turned and stumbled to the back of the rows of people and curled up in the grass to let the sun soak onto her skin as she cried, trying to disappear from the reality that was breaking her heart. The preacher continued on with the service, but her ears felt as though they were bleeding at the words, and she tried to drown out the noise with her own intense crying, and after a little while she removed her little black gloves to wipe her tears, allowing the harshness of the day's event to hit her as she heard him call Willis up to the front to say a few words. Her sobs worsened.

"James Hunter was the best man I ever knew. He was my closest friend, like a brother to me. We did everything together. Well, that was until he met that beautiful lady he called his wife, who was his everything."

"James..." she whispered softly, "Just say it isn't so. I feel like my heart is breaking."

Several minutes later, the people began to sing and she allowed the music to lull her into a light sleep, until she was awakened by the sound of the twenty-one-gun salute, and each shot felt like it was piercing her heart with each startling fire that rang out.

"Mrs. Hunter."

She looked up to the stiffly dressed military man as he presented her with a folded-up flag.

"We are so very sorry for your loss and we present you with this flag on behalf of the United States Air Force as a thank you for your husband's service to our country."

He saluted her, as she placed her gloves back on her hands, stood, and wiped the grass off her delicate black dress. Then he gave her the flag as the guns rang out one last time, and she pulled the flag to her chest, checking her heart with the fierce certainty that her husband was dead. But she looked around herself in a daze and tried to imagine that nothing she was seeing was real.

I'm dreaming, she thought. *I have to be. There's no way this can be reality. Life without Jamie? It's not possible. I won't consider it.*

Her breath quickened and she started feeling lightheaded. But her mother escorted her back to the car now.

"We need to get you to the banquet hall. You need to compose yourself," her mother said.

"Why is this about everyone else?!" Melanie yelled. "He's *my* husband!"

"Was... sweetie... *was*. He's gone." Her mother closed the car door and Melanie's grief overtook her as she laid her head on the flag and wept on the back seat.

Melanie didn't want to think of it that way. In her mind, he was still her husband and he always would be, unwilling to face reality.

They arrived to the banquet hall and she walked over to the memorial table that his mother and sisters had set up, with the medals and ribbons awarded to him while he'd served, and all the various pictures of him with his friends and family, but so many pictures of him with her. Immediately, she looked to their wedding picture, picking it up and holding it to her chest, as she looked over the rest of the table, thinking over how she was ever going to survive without him.

She paused on one picture that his mother must've taken from his nightstand, and her thoughts drifted to that night, while she looked over to Janice in the far end of the banquet hall and she wondered how his own mother was managing to keep herself so well collected. Melanie's thoughts couldn't manage to make it past this hour without him, let alone the rest of her life. How could his own mother imagine it?

But her inner turmoil was interrupted when Willis walked up.

"Mel," he hugged her. "Do you need anything? What can I do?"

"I'm not okay, but there's nothing you can do," she sniffled.

"I know," he replied, feeling shamed and thinking that he might've been able to prevent it all.

He looked over to the memorial table at the few pictures there were of them together from their partying days.

"I'm really going to miss that S.O.B.," he said.

Melanie tried to smile, but all she could do was sob harder and lean in to hug him.

"Willis, what am I going to do without him?" she asked.

He sighed and patted her back, "I don't know. I'm gonna miss him too, Mel. He was my only true friend. But you know what? I'll be here whenever you need to get drunk. Okay?"

She sniffled and pulled away, nodding, and he motioned to Amber in distress, who rushed to his rescue.

"How are you holding up?" Amber asked, walking up, rubbing Melanie's arm.

The look on her face said everything, so Amber moved beyond her question. "Why don't I get you something to eat? We have all Jamie's favorites here. What would you like?"

"Did your mom bring that stupid pea salad he likes?"

Amber smiled slightly and nodded.

"I want some of that and bring me Pepsi with lemon."

"You don't drink Pepsi."

"I know," she cried, "But Jamie loves it."

Amber walked away to get the pea salad, knowing it might help Melanie grieve some, and Melanie laid her head down on the table next to his acceptance letter into NASA and held it in her hand whispering, "I'm so mad at you."

Her Mom walked up and resting her hand on Melanie's back, she said, "Harboring bitter feelings against him won't bring him back, sweetie. There's nothing to forgive him for. It's not his fault he died. You need to let yourself grieve."

"Mama, you don't understand because you never loved Daddy like I love Jamie. You never did."

"I'll give you your space." Her mother walked away as Amber was approaching once more.

"Plenty of that terrible pea salad," she said, handing a plate to Melanie, "And I also brought you those pickle chips he liked, with a Pepsi and lemon. Cheer up, honey. He wouldn't want you so distraught."

"I can't get past how everyone is saying everything in past tense; it's too soon for that. I can't face reality." She took a sip of the Pepsi, savoring the taste of lemon, imagining it being the taste that was constantly on Jamie's lips. He loved lemon.

Amber pointed to the picture frame in front of them. "Tell me about that night. You two looked so happy. There's a reason he kept it on his nightstand."

Melanie's eyes filled with tears and she said, "It was that night at the bar; the night he proposed. We were so young." She laid the drink and plate to the side and took the picture and held it tightly to her chest. "He can't be gone," she sobbed. "How did this happen? We had so little time. We needed more time."

"I'm sorry," Amber said. "Life is unfair. Listen sweetie, you sit here and rest while I talk to some relatives. I'll be back in a minute."

Melanie nodded and looked back to James's face because that's all she really wanted was to be able to see his face and she never would again.

"Melanie, the funeral guests are leaving, love," her mother said, as she swirled the pea salad around on her plate, not really feeling the urge to eat anything. "Go say goodbye to his family. They are sad too."

"Yes. You're right."

Wiping her tears, she stood to say goodbye to Janice and Bruce and began apologizing for losing her composure.

"I'm sorry I've been so..."

"Melanie, it's been hard on everyone," Janice said. "Thank you for loving him so passionately and being so faithful to him."

"I want *you* to have the flag," Melanie said.

"Oh, no," Bruce said. "He would've..."

"Please." She handed it to them. "You accepted me and loved me from the day I met you. I want you to keep this piece of him."

"What will you have?" Janice asked.

"Don't be concerned for me. He left me so much, so many memories, pictures, and so much love that could never be replaced." Her sniffling turned to sobs once more and Janice embraced her.

"Sweetie, we know it hurts. I only know the love of a mother, but I know you love him on a deeper level than I could. I'm sorry you didn't get to have him longer. You were so amazing for his life."

Melanie's sobs continued so vehemently that she said, "I'm feeling lightheaded. I think..." She collapsed.

Janice ordered for Bruce to call 911 and then she immediately alerted Melanie's mom, who was busy cleaning up.

"Who is the medical power of attorney?" the doctor asked upon arrival at the hospital.

Melanie's mom looked to the doctor cautiously, "We just came from her husband's funeral. We think that's why she passed out. She was very upset."

"Are you the mother?" the ER doctor asked.

"Yes."

"No children over age 18?"

"No. She's had a few miscarriages though."

"You are next of kin. You are her new medical power of attorney," the doctor responded before asking her to leave the room while he ran a few tests.

Janice and Bruce arrived to the ER a short while later, along with Kaylee, Amber and Greg, also Willis, and they all paced the hall, impatiently waiting to find out if they were going to be burying both of them in the same day. Thankfully, the doctor stepped out just a few moments later.

"She's going to be fine. She hyperventilated herself. But there is something that you should be aware of if she hasn't already told you."

"Is it serious?" her mother asked.

"Well, it's a type of parasite that's been known to cause issues for up to nine months or so. It can cause fatigue, weight gain, and swelling. It can also cause extreme mood swings and heart burn. But don't worry. All we have to do is remove it when it's run its course."

"Well, okay then. DO that," her mother said.

Amber and Kaylee laughed and looked to their mother, who looked to the doctor.

He pulled out a sonogram. "She's about four months pregnant with a baby boy. Congratulations."

Melanie's mother's eyes filled with tears as she stared at the sonogram and Janice burst into tears on her husband's shoulder.

"I understand that this isn't the most pleasant time for a baby since she just lost a husband."

"It's not that, doctor," Kaylee interrupted. "He was an Air Force officer who died tragically and suddenly, and he always wanted a son. This is going to devastate her."

"I see. Well, I can give her the news, or you can. It's up to you."

"I'll tell her." Amber took the sonogram pictures and walked into the room to see Melanie.

"Hey," she said as she situated some pillows to help Melanie sit up. "How are you feeling? You had quite an afternoon."

"Yeah. But all I can think about is pickle jars," she replied.

"Pickle jars?" Amber asked. "That's silly."

Melanie looked to her, eyes filled with tears, and continued, "Yeah, those stupid jars are so hard to open and Jamie always did that for me." She started crying again and laid her head down on the pillow.

Amber ran her fingers through Melanie's hair trying to bring her some comfort, not knowing how to tell her that she was about to have a Jamie Jr.

"Mel, the doctor gave us some news about what happened with you today," Amber explained.

"Oh?" she responded, tilting her head to look in Amber's eyes.

Amber pulled back slightly and cupped her face. "What if I told you that you don't have to live forever without James? And that even though he's gone, he left a piece of himself with you. How would you feel about that?"

"Um, I'm not sure I understand."

Amber pulled out the sonogram, and said, "You have a piece of him right now. The doctor says you're four months pregnant with a baby boy."

"What?! No! It can't be!" she sobbed. "I can't do this alone! This was supposed to be a baby for us together! This isn't fair to him! He *wanted* this son. Life is so unfair. This is his son! He needs to be here for this baby..." She cried heavily against the pillow. "His son needs his daddy."

"I know," Amber tried to comfort as Melanie cried. "Life is unfair."

The next morning, the doctor gave her discharge instructions, but felt that she shouldn't go home alone, so her mother decided to go stay with her.

"Let's get you ready to go home. Okay, love?" her mom said as she gathered their things.

"I can't put that black dress back on. You need to get me something else. I'll never wear that dress again," Melanie said.

"Alright. What would you like? I'll go to your house and get something. It isn't far from here."

"There's a gray t-shirt in my top drawer. It has a big 'Y' and the Bulldogs logo on it. Bring me that and the sweats from his top drawer."

"Of course."

Melanie walked to the window just as it began to rain and her mind drew a blanket of sadness over her once again, so she pulled out the picture of James she had in her purse.

"I miss you," she whispered as she stared at the picture of them from their honeymoon. "I don't know how I'm going to survive without you, Jamie." Staring at his face caused tears to stream down once again, and she feared she would lose control, so she laid down on the hospital bed and pulled up the gown to see if she noticed any change in her stomach size, laying the picture down on her chest.

As she was doing that, the nurse walked in.

"How are you feeling? I need to remove your IV and get you ready to leave."

"Thank you," she replied as the middle-aged nurse started to remove the IV in silence at first, but then began to make conversation.

"I'm so sorry for your loss, dear. If there's anything I can do to help... My dad was a soldier and I think about him every day."

Melanie stopped the nurse after she said that, and with tears in her eyes she asked, "How did you do it?"

"What's that?" she asked.

"How did you move on? How did you heal after losing him?"

"Well, I believe that losing a father is different than a husband, but you never really move on. I think that time just allows someone to understand that life goes on. That person stays with us, they're a part of us, and we grieve, but we never actually get over it, we only learn to handle it better. We realize how to face the day with dignity. Life never teaches us the hard lessons until we have to face them head on. But no one ever teaches us how to cope. We're just thrown into it and expected to do it."

"So, how did *you*?" Melanie asked, wiping her tears.

"I didn't. I was a mess. Allow yourself time to fall apart. Be human. You've lost your husband. Grieve that loss, sweetie. Think about him, remember him, love him, and then when you're finally ready to take a step forward, you'll know. But don't rush yourself, and don't let anyone tell you to let go. Love that man until the day you die. You have that right... There you go," she said, pointing to the bandage on Melanie's arm. "You're all fixed up."

"Thank you for your kind words. I'll never forget them," Melanie said.

Soon after the nurse was finished, her mother returned with the clothes and they left the hospital, driving to Melanie's house.

"I'm going to take a walk," Melanie said as she got out of the car.

"Please don't walk far. I'm concerned for you. Be back in like 10 or 15 minutes, and just circle the block. Okay, love?"

Melanie only nodded, walking away, back facing her mother as she drifted into a trance, letting the cloud covered sky haze her hurting mind.

She walked for miles and miles until she ended up at the one place she wanted most in the world to be— with Jamie. When she approached, her breath escaped her, and she didn't realize how hard it would be to see the sight. But she continued on toward his tombstone, tears soaking her cheeks as she took each step.

When she reached the one etched, "Lieutenant James Tyler Hunter, Husband, Son, Brother 1990-2018," her sobs came so hard that she fell to the ground and laid across the freshly laid dirt, reaching her hand out to touch the marker.

"Jamie!" she cried, "This can't be real!" She pulled herself closer to the tombstone and laid her face on it, digging her fingers into the dirt, "Come back!" she wept. "You have a son! You always wanted a son. He's going to need you. I can't do this on my own!"

After crying all the tears she had left, she listened for any sounds around that someone might be answering her pleas, that there was hope that everything was just a dream. But the only sounds she heard were the cars driving past on the road nearby, and the workers in the graveyard a few spaces away.

"Jamie, you said that you would always be here for me. I need you right now..."

"Melanie," Amber walked up.

Melanie didn't respond but looked up, eyes bloodshot and swollen, and her body covered in dirt.

"Come, sweetie. You don't belong lying here in the dirt. Jamie wouldn't want you out here in the cemetery crying like this. You're pregnant with his son. We both know he would be so angry at you right now."

Melanie wiped her eyes, as Amber laid some flowers next to the tombstone.

Melanie whispered, "You are my whole world... my everything. I'll love you until my last breath." And then she dug her fingers into the dirt once more.

"Let's go. I'm going to be sure that little peanut inside of you is taken care of," Amber said, reaching out, pulling her to stand and Amber took her home for a shower.

"What are you doing?" Amber asked, after Melanie had dressed herself in only his long-sleeved blues shirt and his boxers, and began digging through their bedroom closet, tossing things out.

"I have to find it!" she cried.

"Find what?" Amber asked, walking over, rubbing her hand up Melanie's back, trying to soothe the madness that was erupting from her at that very moment.

"I need to put it back up!" she screamed.

"Melanie, just calm down and tell me what you're looking for. I'm sure I can help."

"No! I need it. I need to have it now because he's gone and I don't have it. I don't have it and he's not ever coming back," she sobbed, collapsing her head onto Amber's shoulder.

"Mel, he is gone. I'm so sorry. I love him too, but I have no idea what your heart is feeling. Now tell me, what is it you're looking for?"

"The poster. When we moved here, he didn't put it up because I asked him not to. Now I need it. I need to look at it every day. I need to see that dreadful, horrible, godawful, damned poster for the rest of my life." She cried as she began digging through the closet again.

Amber stood, reaching onto the top shelf, pulling down a box of James's things that was marked "Yale," and she walked over to the bed, pulling items out one-by-one until she found his poster of Lucy.

"Melanie."

"You found it?" she jumped up and raced over to Amber, who was unrolling the poster.

"Here it is."

Melanie let out a sigh of relief, holding the poster to her chest, and Amber said, "I'll get some tape. You lay down for a rest. Your eyes are so red and swollen."

Melanie laid down but pulled his box close to her, spilling the contents out beside her on the bed so that she could dig through. She found his student pass and smiled at his picture, even though he'd refused to smile for the photo. Rummaging through some more, she saw some grade cards and decided to look at those, noticing he always got A's, and she smiled at that too. Until she got to one where she saw that his grades were some A's, but mostly B's and C's and she was curious about that, but then remembered what Willis had told her...

"He was a mess at school; he couldn't concentrate. He started forgetting assignments, and instead of getting all A's as he used to, he was getting B's, and then C's."

This must've been the semester. Looking at this card brought a surge of love to her heart and a flood of tears to her eyes.

"James," she whispered. "I just want to go back. I want to fix every mistake we made and redo it all. I want to fall in love again... with you... only you... until my last breath."

5 MONTHS LATER

"What will you name him?" the nurse asked as she handed the baby boy to Melanie after a grueling 37 hours of labor, where her mother, Amber, and Janice were sure to be there the whole time.

Melanie looked at his sandy blonde hair, big blue eyes, and long legs, and with a huge smile she declared, "He will be James Tyler Hunter, just like his dad."

Then Janice pulled a package from her things and said, "We got you a present. We thought he might need something to wear." And she showed Melanie the cutest gray onesie with a "Y" and the "Bulldogs" logo, and Melanie knew that James was keeping his promise of always being there for her.

"You look just like your dad, little Jamie. Do you know that?" Melanie told him as she tightly wrapped that baby in her arms and kissed his forehead. "I'm going to love you with all there is of me until the end of my days. With everything I am, I promise that I will not fail you. I will love you until I take my very last breath." Then she closed her eyes and knew that James had given her this one last piece of himself, and she loved him that much more for it.

EPILOGUE

"Where are we, Mommy?" little Jamie asked Melanie as she drove them down to the bridge that overstretched the pond.

"This is somewhere I've always wanted to bring you yet couldn't because it was always too hard for me. This was your daddy's favorite place in the whole world and he brought me here the first night I met him. It was also where we got married," she explained.

Jamie sat down beside her, stretching his long legs over the side, looking up to his mom, watching the tears drip slowly from her eyes.

"Don't be sad. I'm sure my daddy is watching us right now, and I'm glad you brought me here today, Mommy. What did you talk about when my daddy brought you here that night you met him?" Jamie asked, looking out across the pond, watching the frogs hop from one place to another.

"Well, your daddy really liked me a lot, so he wanted to get to know me. He asked me about my family, and I asked him about what he was studying at his college."

"You mean his airplanes?" Jamie wondered.

"Yes. All those planes and rockets you play with every day were all because your daddy wanted to be a pilot for NASA," Melanie said.

"Was he a good pilot?"

"Yeah, Jamie. He was," she said, sighing.

"Is that why you liked him?" he asked.

"Well, I didn't even know he was a pilot at the time. I think I liked your daddy because I knew there was something special about him. He was special just as you are special. And he was

248

smart. I knew from the moment I met him that he was going to challenge me every day, just like you do." She winked to Jamie.

"He was *very* smart. That's what Nana Janice says. But Auntie Amber tells me that Daddy was always tellin' her what to do. That he was nothin' but a smarty pants."

"Heh. Yeah. Nana Janice is right. I always told your daddy that he was a genius, which he was, but he never believed it. Auntie Amber was probably getting told because she was doing naughty things."

"You're right about Auntie Amber. She is always doin' naughty things. Mommy? Do you think I'm smart enough to be a pilot like my daddy?"

"Absolutely, baby. And I know he'd be very proud of that. You're the one thing in life he wanted but never got."

"Well, he's got me right now. I talk to him every night before I go to sleep," he said.

"You do?" she asked.

"Yep," Jamie answered.

"What else do you do that I don't know about?" she asked, looking over to him as he leaned his head over the wooden railing to peer into the water.

"Not much. But I talk to Daddy ever since you gave me his picture on my dresser. I tell him how I wish I knew him and how I like that I have his blue eyes and not your brown eyes. I also tell him that I want to be a pilot and an engineer someday just like him. But I told him that Uncle Willis tells me all the bad things he used to do."

"You know what? I'm sure he's listening, and I think that he'd be okay with you talking about those things with your Uncle Willis too."

"You do?" he asked, glancing back to Melanie just slightly.

"Yep. Uncle Willis and your daddy were the best of buds back then. They used to do everything together before I married your daddy and before Uncle Willis married Aunt Kay. Back then, it was always Uncle Willis and James. Like how it is with you and your cousin Tobie."

"Yeah, well, Tobie can be a trouble stirrer like Aunt Kay."

Melanie laughed. "I know. But your daddy would be so happy to see Uncle Will with her and to know that they have a little boy, but also to see that you are good buddies with him."

After thinking on that thought for a moment, Melanie was finding it hard to hold back her tears, so she pointed to a few frogs along the grass line and told Jamie to try to catch one to take home for his aquarium. Once he was distracted, she pulled out a letter from her pocket that she'd been keeping in her nightstand for the past six years.

When James died, he'd left her a large sum of life insurance money to be sure her needs were met until she figured out what to do for herself in the event of his death. Knowing that James would've wanted her to, she went to college and got a degree in nursing, hoping to be able to care for patients just like James, and wives just like her.

But the letter was written to her in James's handwriting and was given to her with the life insurance paperwork, which she'd figured was just something he drafted with their decision to get married and James thinking she needed to be told how to spend the money. However, she refused to open it, feeling like it was her one last connection, one last piece of him. Nearly six years later, graduated from college, watching little Jamie look more and more like his dad every day, she was finally ready to take the leap and read what James wrote in the insurance paperwork, remembering what the nurse had said to her all those years prior...

"That person stays with us, they're a part of us, and we grieve, but we never actually get over it, we only handle it better. We learn to face the day with dignity... Allow yourself time to fall apart. Be human. You've lost your husband. Grieve that loss, sweetie. Think about him, remember him, love him, and then when you're finally ready to take a step forward, you'll know. But don't rush yourself, and don't let anyone tell you to let go. Love that man until the day you die. You have that right."

She looked down to little Jamie, smiled at his likeness of his father, and opened the letter...

Melanie,

My most beautiful wife, I'm beginning this letter by stating its purpose because I know what it means to be entering into NASA and I knew what it meant to sign up for the Air Force. I was prepared for that, but I wasn't ever certain if you were. For that, I thank you for always being there for me and supporting me through everything. You are amazing. I've never deserved you.

I've written you this letter because I know the risks I've chosen in life and because I know the choices and decisions that lay ahead, I don't want to miss the opportunity to say what could've been said while I had the moment. Three things I want you to know:

1. You're the most important thing in all of life to me. Not my planes, not my career, nothing is more important than you.

2. From the moment I saw you, I knew I wanted to marry you. It is because of this letter that I didn't right away. Because I knew that someday my life decisions could be making you a widow.

3. You were always too good for me. I know you believed it the other way around, but you need to know your value, Melanie Hunter. You are so precious, and when I look at you, I see the beauty that no rare gem could ever match. I love you.

If you're reading this, it's because my choices brought me an ill-timed death. Because of that, the first thing I want you to understand is that with all of my heart, with all of my soul, with all of there is of me, I love you. You were the spark that ignited every flame of life inside my soul. I needed you. I didn't know it until I had you, but the universe knew it and sent you to me.

We were meant to be. You saved me from the wrong path in life. Thank you for being everything any man could possibly need in a mate. I couldn't have asked for more.

Next, I need to say that I'm sorry. I'm sorry that the life I chose brought you this letter. I'm sorry for everything I ever did wrong. I'm sorry that I'm not there with you now. I'm sorry for every time that you'll need me and I won't be there to help you. I'm sorry for not listening to you when you asked me to stay. I'm sorry for it all. I wish I could make all the bad go away and just give you good, but I can't, not now. All I can do now is just ask you to know how regretful I am for every piece of my life that I've ever done wrong. Forgive me, Melanie. You are my whole world. I'll love you until my very last breath.

The last thing is that I hope you're happy. Don't spend your days lonely. I know you. I know your heart. I know you're moping around missing me. But I also know that you know me well enough to know that isn't what I want. Follow your dreams. Reach for the stars. Do it for me. I love you now and always. Thank you for making my life complete.

Your husband- the man who loves you more than anyone else,

James

She cried for a minute over his words and then she looked to little Jamie playing in the water, catching frogs, and she realized something about the letter— it was dated one day prior to his death. He'd arranged the letter and the life insurance having not even received his acceptance letter into NASA yet, and she wondered over what spurred him into arranging the letter and insurance information if he hadn't even known he was accepted into NASA. Then she remembered the morning he died, and he told her that they'd received a new jet. She looked to the wedding rings on her fingers, and she realized that he must've known that there was a chance...

"I'm very useful to them..." she remembered him saying the morning of his accident, and her heart felt anguished as little Jamie ran up to her, holding the frog he caught, with a huge smile on his face.

"I got one!" he yelled out.

"Let's see him," Melanie said.

Jamie opened his hands and just as he did, the frog hopped off his hands and onto the bridge, then back into the water.

Melanie smiled and patted the area on the bridge next to her for Jamie to sit down.

"Why are you crying?" he asked.

"I was reading a sad letter," she answered.

"Can I hear it?" he asked.

"Maybe when you're older," she replied.

"Do you miss Daddy?" he asked her, as he watched her wipe the tears dripping down her face.

"Very much," she said.

"Are you thinking about him right now?" he asked.

"Yeah," she answered.

"What are you thinking about?"

"I'm thinking about what a good man he was, and about how much he loved me, but also about how much he wanted you." She leaned in and kissed Jamie's forehead, brushing his sandy blonde hair away from his eyes.

"Can we go visit him today?" Jamie asked, as Melanie stood and reached down, helping him to a stand.

"Yeah. I think that'd be good," she replied, smiling and wiping her tears.

"Can we take him a new a plane?" Jamie asked, jumping enthusiastically.

"Of course we can. He would love that."

Then they walked back to the truck and drove to the one place in the whole world they both wanted most to be— with James.

Thank you for your purchase and I hope you enjoyed the book! Be sure to leave a review on Amazon and join my mailing list on www.AuthorMegsechrest.com to be the first to know about new releases and special book deals and author events. Connect with me on Twitter and Instagram @Megswritesbooks. Turn the page to check out the preview of an upcoming release...

Coming Soon...

"Melanie?" Amber said, stepping into the room.

"You have a visitor," the nurse said, walking in behind Amber.

"Are you staying?" Amber asked the nurse.

"Yes. She isn't permitted visitors without supervision. Her psychiatrist believes her to be a risk."

"A risk?" Amber asked.

"Your sister-in-law believes her husband, who has been dead for 19 years, is somehow still alive. She is severely mentally unstable. We cannot allow your lives to be put into harm's way." He walked to the far corner and stood with his arms crossed, watching Melanie's every move, while Amber and Willis and Kaylee approached Melanie, Amber sitting down next to her on the bed.

"Mel..." Amber said.

"He's alive," Melanie said, as Amber laid her arm on Melanie's shoulder. "I know he is. I can *feel* it."

"Melanie," Amber said. "He's gone. He's been gone for 19 years, sweetie. The doctors say that you've been having some disturbing dreams. You want to tell us about those?"

"No!" Melanie snapped.

"Melanie," Kaylee said, "We are here to help you. We know that life raising Jamie on your own has been so hard. We all love you so much. We know James did too."

"I wish he was here again too," Willis said. "No one's ever meant more in life to me than my family and that guy. I want to help. But you need to *let* us help you."

"Just stop!" she screamed, grabbing and pulling at her hair, tucking her legs in close to her chest. "All of you! Get out! Just go!"

"Melanie, just talk to me. I'm your best friend and your sister..." Amber pleaded.

"Get away from me!" she screamed again. "You don't understand!"

"I'm trying to understand. Help me understand," Amber begged.

Melanie started smacking at Amber's hands, pushing her away, kicking her back, yelling, "Go away! Leave! You aren't here to help me. You want to take him from me! You are just like them! You want to give me that medicine to take him away from me!"

The nurse hurried over, pulling Melanie back, grabbing her arms behind her back, holding her still.

"I need 5 mg of Haldol stat," the nurse said to his talkie as he was holding Melanie still, who was fighting to break free.

Amber began crying as she watched Melanie struggle against the large male nurse's grip, while he held her down and gave her the shot of calming medication and Melanie kept shouting, "He isn't dead! You don't know what you are doing! I'm not crazy!"

(Excerpt taken from BREATH ESCAPES ME- sequel to My Last Breath. Expected Release: Spring 2019)

Acknowledgments

First, I want to thank my husband, without whom none of this would be possible. Kevin, I love you, and I thank you for all the extra things you do. You are an extraordinary person, and I am so grateful to be your wife.

To my children, thank you for surrendering your mother for hours, days, and weeks on end for something that you are not even allowed to read, yet. Bribery wins. Always.

Carrie, you are my biggest fan, and throughout my writing adventure, you have graciously given me advice, tips, encouragement, and so much friendly inspiration that I couldn't have finished this without you! Thank you for being there!

Lola, thank you for all the beautiful images you design and create so willingly. You are very talented and I am blessed to work with you! Here's to many more designs and books and many more days of putting up with me!

To my other readers, Candace, Crystal, Aunt Tammy, and my betas on social! Thank you for your time, energy, and support. Your encouragement and effort means so much to me.

To my models, Kate and Brandon Egebrecht, and Chris Rassel. Thank you for your patience and cooperation as we tried numerous times to get just the right pose! You look fabulous!

Lastly, but most certainly not least, I want to thank God, who whispered in my ear that I was strong enough to keep going when the devil kept telling me that I wasn't. Isaiah 41:10, Exodus 14:14, and Deuteronomy 31:8.

16461029R00154

Made in the USA
Middletown, DE
24 November 2018